English for academic study:

UNIVERSITY OF PLYMOUTH
ENGLISH LANGUAGE CENTRE

Extended Writing & Research Skills

Teacher's Book

Joan McCormack and John Slaght

University of **Reading**

CALS
Centre for Applied Language Studies

Garnet
EDUCATION

Credits

Published by
Garnet Publishing Ltd.
8 Southern Court
South Street
Reading RG1 4QS, UK

This edition first published 2005
Reprinted 2006, 2008
Fully revised 2009

ISBN: 978 1 85964 503 1

British Cataloguing-in-Publication Data
A catalogue record for this book is available from
the British Library.

Production
Project manager: Simone Davies
Project consultant: Rod Webb
Editorial team: Penny Analytis, Jo Caulkett,
                      Simone Davies, Chris Gough,
                      Fiona McGarry
Design and layout: Mike Hinks, Sarah Church

Every effort has been made to trace the copyright
holders and we apologize in advance for any
unintentional omission. We will be happy to insert the
appropriate acknowledgements in any subsequent
editions.

Printed and bound In Lebanon by International Press

Contents

i Introduction — Page 7

1 Introduction to the skills of extended writing and research — Page 17

2 Using evidence to support your ideas — Page 25

3 Structuring your project and finding information — Page 33

4 Developing your project — Page 39

5 Developing a focus — Page 45

6 Introductions, conclusions and definitions — Page 55

7 Incorporating data and illustrations — Page 73

8 Preparing for conference presentations and editing your work — Page 81

a Appendices:

Appendix 1: Written project evaluation — Page 86
Appendix 2: Presentation assessment — Page 89

Book map

Topic	Tasks

1 Introduction to the skills of extended writing and research

- Critical thinking in academic study
- What do students in higher education write?
- Types of writing
- Participating in a tutorial: getting help with writing
- Analyzing the task
- The stages of writing a project
- Starting Project 1: ideas for the introduction, main body and conclusion
- Unit Summary

2 Using evidence to support your ideas

- Selective reading: reading for research purposes
- Incorporating evidence into academic work
- Referencing: direct quotations, summaries and paraphrases
- Purposeful reading: searching texts for definitions
- Features of a summary
- Stages in writing a summary or paraphrase
- Practice summary 1
- Practice summary 2
- Practice summary 3
- Unit Summary

3 Structuring your project and finding information

- The structure of projects
- Descriptive and evaluative writing
- Reading for a specific purpose
- Choosing sources
- Finding information
- Analyzing websites: critical evaluation
- Acknowledging your sources
- Academic conventions in referencing
- When to avoid using online sources
- Writing a bibliography
- Unit Summary

4 Developing your project

- Preparing for tutorials: discussing feedback on draft text
- Quotations, paraphrases and plagiarism
- Avoiding plagiarism
- Working with abstracts
- Unit Summary

5 Developing a focus

- Choosing a topic for your extended essay
- Developing a topic
- Establishing a focus
- Establishing a working title
- Planning Project 2
- Unit Summary

Topic	Tasks
6 Introductions, conclusions and definitions	• Features of introductions
	• Analyzing your introduction
	• The language of introductions
	• Identifying the thesis statement
	• Features of conclusions
	• Analyzing your conclusion
	• The language of conclusions
	• Features of definitions
	• Unit Summary
7 Incorporating data and illustrations	• The purpose of data
	• The language used for incorporating data
	• Data commentary
	• The language of data commentary
	• Practice data commentary
	• Unit Summary
8 Preparing for conference presentations and editing your work	• Features of abstracts
	• Conference abstracts
	• Preparing an oral presentation
	• Preparing a poster presentation
	• Unit Summary

Acknowledgements

The creation of these materials stemmed from the need to help international students develop the study skills necessary to function effectively on academic courses in a university context. The rationale behind the material is that students need to develop the confidence and competence to become autonomous learners in order to successfully carry out research and complete assignments, such as extended pieces of written work, or to give oral presentations.

The development of these materials has been a collaborative effort which goes far beyond the collaboration between the authors. The material has evolved over several years of pre-sessional teaching at the Centre for Applied Language Studies at the University of Reading. There have been significant additions from a number of teachers, who have either contributed ideas or given extensive feedback on the materials. The number of teachers involved is too large for us to mention each one individually, but they are all fully appreciated.

In something like their present form, the materials have been trialled on successive pre-sessional courses at the University of Reading since 2001. This trialling has involved almost a thousand students, and they too have provided feedback in terms of course evaluation, as well as with their responses to the tasks in the programme. We very much appreciate the contribution of students whose work has been adapted and incorporated into the materials.

We would like to thank Bruce Howell for his contributions to the development of the accompanying online tasks.

Particular mention should also be made of the contribution of our colleague, Sarah Brewer, for her ideas selflessly shared, her knowledge of referencing and academic conventions and her patient and meticulous editing – not to mention the seven years she has spent teaching and commenting upon the contents of this book.

Joan McCormack and John Slaght, authors, June 2009

Introduction

EAS Extended Writing & Research Skills has been designed with the aims of helping students to:

● improve their extended writing and research skills;
● develop an independent approach to extended writing and research.

Principles and approach

Aims of the course

The purpose of this course is to equip students with the skills necessary for conducting research and for producing a piece of extended writing (referred to here as a project) in their own subject-specific area. The course involves an integrated approach, with a particular focus on the writing and research skills necessary for such a task. The course is designed to encourage *critical thinking* and get students to be *evaluative* in their approach to writing. There is also a strong oral component to the course, through discussion of the students' work in class and in tutorials, and at the end of the course, when students practise preparing for a conference presentation.

It is assumed that discrete reading and writing skills, as well as presentation skills, are taught in other components of an English for Academic Purposes course. For example, although students will be asked to consider the structure of introductions and conclusions, it will be assumed that they are already familiar with this to some degree. Similarly, although students receive language feedback on their work, they are not explicitly taught grammar in these materials.

Student needs

The following areas have been taken into consideration in the design of the materials, based on an analysis of what students will need to do on future courses:
• the ability to produce an extended piece of writing in their own subject area, within the academic conventions of higher education in the West;
• the development of discursive skills – to communicate effectively both orally and in writing;
• the development of critical thinking skills;
• the development of learner autonomy;
• an understanding of the conventions of the academic community students will typically be joining;
• the development and consolidation of study competencies.

Principles on which the materials are based

The learning process as a cycle
Mayes (1999) examines how different learning activities enhance students' understanding of new concepts and resolve misunderstandings. He refers to three stages, which are known as the *conceptualisation cycle*.

At the *conceptualisation stage*, students are exposed to the ideas or concepts of others through lectures, reading and seminar discussion. During the *construction stage*, students apply these new concepts in the performance of meaningful tasks. It is during the *dialogue stage*, however, that learning takes place through the performance of tasks, when these new concepts are tested during written communication and/or conversation with tutors and peers. The feedback provided enables students' misconceptions to be resolved. The approach adopted by these materials is based on similar principles.

Also, the integration of skills from other components of a typical EAP course is an essential aspect of the project preparation class. Students bring with them awareness of the micro-skill of writing and an awareness of how to use appropriate reading strategies to deal with texts. These are aspects which are recycled in the project class. In this context, writing is learnt rather than taught, because learning how to write occurs through the understanding and manipulation of content.

Reading for the purpose of writing: writing from multiple texts

The approach taken in these materials is that students are reading to learn, rather than learning to read. To encourage this, students are given a reading purpose: to complete a project (an extended writing assignment). This purpose should generate a 'selective' reading approach, which will help students to deal with the literally hundreds of pages they may be confronted with each week during their future academic courses. It is also generally accepted that teaching students to write from sources is essential preparation for academic success. In his book on the relationship between reading and writing, Grabe points out the complexity of the process, which involves deciding: how much and which material should be used; how it can be used in relation to the task; how accurately it should be represented; and, finally, the formal mechanisms that need to be used (Grabe, 2003, p. 225).

The process and problem-solving components of writing development can make intense demands on students, particularly when they are reading difficult L2 texts in order to collect or glean new information for their writing. In many reading-writing tasks, students are forced to make a number of complex decisions (Grabe, 2001, p. 245).

It is with this in mind that students are given a range of sources to consider when working on Project 1. The rationale behind this approach is that the teacher has an element of control and can identify ineffective strategies that students may be tempted to employ as a way of coping with multiple, fairly dense academic texts, such as varying degrees of plagiarism.

With Project 2, students will be working with texts in their own subject area and with a much greater degree of autonomy. By this stage, it is hoped that they will have begun to develop the ability to make the 'complex decisions' that Grabe identifies.

A process and product approach

A process approach to writing is advocated, based on research which shows that the process of doing helps the development of organization as well as meaning. It is expected that writing skills will be taught elsewhere, but further development occurs through the process of students completing their project, through drafting and redrafting their work. At each stage of writing, students are encouraged and expected to generate ideas, organize them, evaluate what they are writing and identify clearly what their writing purpose is. Revision is essential, not just to edit the language, but also to reorganize or modify the text and clarify ideas, as necessary, through expansion or rephrasing. At every stage of the process, students are encouraged to critically assess what they have written and to develop this criticality through discussion with their academic colleagues, whether fellow students or teachers.

These materials also strongly emphasize the importance of the end product. This is in line with the needs of students on their future academic courses, when they will have to produce an end product containing some or all of the aspects of academic writing and academic study skills advocated in these materials. Please refer to Appendix 1 at the end of this Teacher's Book for an example of how the written project may be evaluated, taking into account not only the content, the use of source materials, the organization and the language of the final draft, but also the actual written presentation of the text and the degree of learner independence exercised by students in producing the final product.

Students finding their own voice

In the complexity of the reading and writing process, students often find it challenging to formulate their own ideas. A strong element of these materials involves getting students to clarify their ideas by voicing them before writing them down. It is important to emphasize to students that even though they are writing in their own subject area, they should be writing with the educated reader in mind, i.e., they should be able to explain their topic to others.

One of the reasons that students plagiarize is that they want to use information they have read to support a point without having fully understood the text. Verbalizing their ideas before writing helps combat this to some extent by helping them clarify their understanding before beginning to write. Students are provided with the texts for Project 1, and are asked to be critical from the beginning. They may be resistant to this approach if they come from a culture where they are not expected to question authoritative sources.

Learner autonomy

Students are expected to be independent learners in higher education. They need to work not only on their study skill techniques, e.g., note-taking and compiling a bibliography, but also on acquiring study competencies which involve the development of critical questioning. Control over one's learning is the basis of learner autonomy; not only attempting to do it but also actually managing it successfully. However, student attitudes to working autonomously vary in terms of their cultural background, as well as according to the personality of the individual.

The stage of learner autonomy of any student will always be at a certain point along a continuum. The current materials therefore contain 'scaffolded' tasks which provide support throughout much of the course, but which are gradually withdrawn to encourage autonomy, especially during the writing of Project 2. In their article on issues in the EAP curriculum, Flowerdew and Peacock emphasize the importance of this. By asking learners to research and investigate resources available to them inside and outside the academy, as well as encouraging learners to take responsibility for their own learning, teachers will set their students on the path to full independence (Flowerdew & Peacock, 2001, p. 82).

Using *EAS Extended Writing & Research Skills*

Unit Summaries

These provide an opportunity for the students to reflect on what they have done at the end of each unit. You may wish students to complete the unit summaries in class or in their own time. If they complete them out of class, make sure you find time to discuss what the students have done.

The appendices

There are eight units in total, plus the appendices. Each unit focuses on one aspect of extended writing. When to employ the appendices most usefully is suggested in the table on page 10.

Appendix	Content	When to use
1	Sample project	Unit 3, Tasks 1.1 and 1.2. However, some teachers may prefer to introduce the project during the very first class so that students get an impression of what the final product should be.
2	Self-evaluation checklist	This is probably best introduced in Unit 2, possibly before or after Task 4, as a homework task. As suggested in the instructions on page 119 of the Course Book, students should be encouraged to visit this self-evaluation checklist at appropriate stages throughout their course in order to reflect on their progress. Discussing the checklist could form part of their tutorial time.
3	Advice on note-taking	Unit 2 specifically, but students should be encouraged to refer to this appendix at each stage of their note-taking for Projects 1 and 2, e.g., in Unit 4, with reference to avoiding plagiarism.
4 (4.1–4.6)	Sources for Project 1	These should be introduced in Unit 2, when students begin work on Project 1; also during Unit 3, Task 4, in relation to critical reading.
5	Compiling a bibliography	Unit 3 (pages 44–48), which deals with acknowledging sources and academic conventions in referencing. Unit 4 covers the tutorial system and avoiding plagiarism, and teachers may find it more appropriate to introduce the compilation of a bibliography at this point, or even later in the materials.

Other features

Glossary: This contains a useful list of terms that the students will need to know during the course.

Study tips: These contain additional information that can be used by the students as a ready reference to a range of study issues related to extended writing and research skills.

Web resources: There are suggested web resources at the end of each unit. These provide further areas of practice or study on topics or skills related to the unit.

Interactive online activities: Additional interactive activities can be found at www.englishforacademicstudy.com. These form an important part of the materials, as they support the material in each unit and are aimed at encouraging students to develop an independent approach to academic work. The website should also help familiarize students with how to carry out a range of online activities and access online resources. This is increasingly expected of students in the higher education system in the West.

You may decide to schedule the tasks outlined in the table on page 11 as homework assignments, or leave it to the students' discretion to carry out the tasks at appropriate stages during the course. Whatever the case, it would be useful to copy the table below and distribute it to the students for their information.

Online activities schedule

Unit	Website activity	Where used
1	The structure of a project Using the library	after Task 3, page 12 end of the unit
2	Referencing in a text	after Task 3, page 24
3	Evaluating Internet sources Bibliographies	after Task 6, page 43 after Task 10, page 48
4	Avoiding plagiarism	after Task 3, page 54
5	Focus on essay titles Successful searching How to evaluate a website	after Task 3, page 63 after Task 5, page 67
6	Introductions Conclusions	after Task 7, page 79
7	Describing data Interpreting data	after Task 5, page 92
8	How to prepare a presentation Evaluating presentations	after Task 3, page 99

Issues

There are certain issues relating to these materials and how they are introduced and used on an EAP course. One issue which needs to be considered is the academic experience and cultural background of the students involved. Secondly, their level of intellectual maturity has to be considered. Both of these issues will impact on the amount of scaffolding which should be given and possibly the extent to which Project 1 should form part of the overall assessment.

Completing Projects 1 and 2

If students follow the whole course, then they are expected to write both Project 1 and Project 2.

Project 1 (about 1,200 words) is carefully scaffolded, and the sources that the students use for their topic are included in the appendices. Units 1–4 of the book introduce a range of extended writing and research skills which can be practised *during* the completion of this first project; in other words, students are working on Project 1 in parallel with working on the earlier units. It is up to the teacher to decide when to get them started – it could be within the first week. The completion of Project 1 means that students are putting into practice the skills they are developing through working on the earlier units.

For Project 1
- The emphasis is not on teaching writing, but on students putting into practice and consolidating the writing skills they have already been taught.
- Texts are supplied, but students are still expected to use two resources of their own, providing a challenge for stronger students.
- Students are asked to select from a limited number of texts.
- The structure and mechanics are introduced while the project is being written.
- The writing also involves synthesis: bringing together ideas from a range of sources.

The aim then is for students to work on Project 2 (2,000–3,000 words), in their own academic subject area, and for them to develop their independent learning skills while using and consolidating the skills already introduced during the completion of Project 1. Unit 5 should be used to introduce Project 2, and teachers can decide to return to certain tasks covered or passed over earlier if necessary for revision and further consolidation. Teachers might decide to include Unit 6 as part of Project 1, or to wait until the introduction of the second project. Although students will be expected to be more autonomous by this stage, whole class tasks could be attempted from Units 7 and 8, as appropriate. Teachers need to decide whether their students will complete Project 1 before moving on to Project 2, in the individual student's academic area. This will depend on factors such as the length of the course, the number of hours per week dedicated to extended writing and research skills, the level and needs of the students and their previous tertiary level experience.

For Project 2
- Students look for and use their own resources in their own subject area.
- Students negotiate their own title and specific aim through dialogue with their personal tutor.
- Scaffolding is withdrawn, and students work more independently.
- Class time is mainly concentrated on individual tutorials.
- Students are encouraged to take responsibility for what happens in the tutorial, and guidance on this is given in Unit 4 (pages 50–51).

Completing Project 2 only

If students do not need to do Project 1, or if there is insufficient time, teachers are advised to make decisions about a route through the materials depending on the particular circumstances of their programme. For example, if there is only sufficient time to complete Project 2, then consideration should be given to following the route suggested on pages 15–16 of this book, which proposes that Unit 5 is introduced very early on. This particular route is based on allocation of 30 hours over a 6-week period. It includes preparation for a conference/oral presentation about an aspect of the students' projects, which may be inappropriate for some EAP courses. In such cases, time allocated for this in the suggested route could be channelled into another aspect of the material.

Feedback and assessment

Assessment includes both continuous assessment and assessment of the written project(s), as well as the presentation (Appendices 1 and 2 in the Teacher's Book provide the evaluation criteria for these).

Each of the units contains a number of tasks, many of which students could complete outside class time, to be checked in class. Parallel to this, students are working on their projects, and get feedback on each stage of the process, e.g., on their initial plan, or on whether the introduction contains a clear focus. Although they may be familiar with the process of peer evaluation in the writing component of their course, the extent to which it is a part of the process of the project class varies according to the individual group. Ideally, it should happen, but if a group is struggling with both the content and the structure of the project, it may be too demanding to expect students to also be involved in effective peer feedback. However, a great deal can be gained from using colleagues as 'sounding boards' to try out ideas and to explain the content as clearly and effectively as possible.

Students should receive both formative and summative feedback on their written drafts of the project from the teacher, and have the opportunity to discuss their work in an individual tutorial. Certain aspects of feedback sessions are particularly significant, for example, written comments on the final project as well as the drafts. Students also need feedback on their oral performance in preparation for their conference presentation. On longer courses, it is often possible to organize 'mock' tutorials as part of the students' spoken language assessment. To make this a more authentic experience, the students' projects can be used as the focus for discussion. Students can be asked to introduce their project, outline the key details and then discuss issues relating to their project with the assessor.

Referencing

The system of referencing used in the materials is that of the APA (American Psychological Association). See a brief summary in Appendix 5 of the Course Book.

A number of the sources included have used different systems; these have been reproduced in the original form. It is worth pointing this out to students, and ensuring they follow the APA system consistently in their own writing of projects.

However, individual institutions or groups may well have their own system. It is important to be systematic and meticulous in the choice and use of the system decided on. Obviously it is not possible to move between different systems.

Plagiarism

This is described as a "sticky issue – not seen as black and white by academics" (Sutherland Smith, 2005). For example, there is the need to "imitate in the early stages of learning a new discourse" (Angelil-Carter, 2000). On the other hand, as expressed by Sherman (1992, p. 194), "they (the students) find it hard to believe that I really want what I say I want: their own half-formed ideas expressed in their own limited English."

Some students feel that they are representing the writer more fairly by using her/his words. However, the materials aim to raise awareness and develop the skills/techniques to help overcome plagiarism. There is a strong emphasis on being evaluative and on students 'commenting' on what they have read. There is also an attempt to help students develop the skills to be able to express ideas effectively.

References

Angelil-Carter, S. (2000). *Stolen language?: plagiarism in writing*. New York: Longman.

Flowerdew, J. & Peacock, M. (2001). The EAP curriculum: Issues, methods and challenges. In J. Flowerdew & M. Peacock (Eds.), *Research perspectives on English for Academic Purposes*. Cambridge: CUP.

Grabe, N. (2003). Reading and writing relations: second language perspectives on research and practice. In B. Kroll (Ed.), *Exploring the dynamics of second language writing*. Cambridge: CUP.

Lynch, T. (2001). Promoting EAP learner autonomy in a second language university context. In J. Flowerdew & M. Peacock (Eds.), *Research perspectives on English for Academic Purposes*. Cambridge: CUP.

Mayes, J.T. & Fowler, C.F.H. (1999). Learning technology and usability: a framework for understanding courseware. *Interacting with computers, 11*, 185-497.

Robinson, P., Strong, G., Whittle, J. & Nobe, S. (2001). The development of EAP oral discussion ability. In J. Flowerdew & M. Peacock (Eds.), *Research perspectives on English for Academic Purposes*. Cambridge: CUP.

Sherman, J. (1992). Your own thoughts in your own words. *ELT Journal 46*(2), pp. 190–198.

Sutherland Smith, W. & Carr, R. (2005). Turnitin.com: teachers' perspectives of anti-plagiarism software in raising issues of educational integrity. *Journal of University Teaching & Learning Practice, 2*(3), article 10.

Water, A. & Waters, M. (2003). Designing tasks for the development of study competencies. In B. Kroll (Ed.), *Exploring the dynamics of second language writing*. Cambridge: CUP.

Route through the materials

This book is intended to cover, for example, a ten-week course (one whole academic term) of approximately four to five contact hours per week plus homework. It is assumed that the core micro-skills of writing are dealt with in another component of the course, e.g., writing introductions and conclusions. This book does not aim to teach these micro-skills, but rather to reinforce them.

On a full-time course, students could be using the *Reading* and *Writing* books from the EAS series during the morning sessions, for example, and working on the *Extended Writing & Research Skills* materials in the afternoons. The rationale behind this is that students then develop their skills during the *Reading* and *Writing* sessions and put them into practice during the *Extended Writing & Research Skills* sessions.

For ten-week courses, for example, one unit per week should be covered, based on four 90-minute periods per week. However, it may only take nine weeks to cover the actual material, and students will spend the rest of their time working on their own projects. The final weeks will be mainly individual tutorials, with little class input, as students will be working independently.

It is assumed that students completing a course of eight weeks or more will complete all units of the book and tasks to suit their needs. On pages 15–16 is a suggested route for students undertaking a course of six weeks or fewer. It is based on the assumption that they will have six hours of tuition per week.

The course book is supplemented by additional interactive activities at www.englishforacademicstudy.com. Students should be encouraged to work on these materials, either for homework or as self-study support work.

Note: On a short course, it is important to explain the purpose of the project preparation class in the first lesson. Explain that the tasks are designed to help the students develop the skills they need. It is also important to explain that the materials have been designed for much longer courses, so some of the contents may be omitted; point out, for example, that they will only be writing Project 2 (in their subject area). Finally, explain that some of the work may not follow the order of the book.

Date	Lesson content	Homework
Week 1 (Session 1)	• Explain aims and objectives of the project class • CB Unit 1, Task 6 (pages 15–16): *The stages of writing a project* **Note:** Remember to give out written language assignment for students to complete for negotiated deadline.	• CB Appendix 2 (pages 119–120): *Self-evaluation checklist* • Read through Unit 1 for consolidation • Students search for sources in their subject area
(Session 2)	• Briefly refer to self-evaluation checklist in Appendix 2 (pages 119–120) • CB Unit 5, Introduction and Task 1 (page 62): *Choosing a topic for your extended essay* • CB Unit 5, Task 3 (pages 63–64): *Establishing a focus* • CB Unit 5, Task 4 (pages 65–66): *Establishing a working title*	
(Session 3)	• CB Unit 2, Tasks 2 and 3 (pages 23–26): *Incorporating evidence into academic work; Referencing*	• Complete unfinished work from Unit 2, Tasks 2 and 3 • Research for project ongoing
Week 2 (Session 1)	• CB Unit 3, Task 1 (pages 33–35). *The structure of projects* • CB Unit 3, Task 2 (pages 36–37) *Descriptive and evaluative writing*	• CB Unit 3, Task 5 (pages 39–43): *Finding information.* Students should read carefully for negotiated deadline and complete the task.
(Session 2)	• CB Unit 3, Task 10 (page 48): *Writing a bibliography*	• Planning and making notes for first draft
(Session 3)	• CB Unit 4, Tasks 2 and 3 (pages 52–55): *Quotations, paraphrases and plagiarism; Avoiding plagiarism*	• Writing first draft
(Session 4)	• Unit 6, Introduction and Task 1 (pages 70–72): *Features of introductions*	• Writing first draft (to be submitted by negotiated deadline)
Week 3 (Session 1)	• Tutorials	• Students respond to tutorial comments
(Session 2)	• Tutorials	• Students respond to tutorial comments
(Session 3)	• CB Unit 6, Tasks 5–7 (pages 75–79): *Features of conclusions; Analyzing your conclusion; The language of conclusions*	• CB Unit 7 (pages 84–93) Students should read contents of the unit and complete Task 3 (page 90): *Data commentary.*
Week 4 (Session 1)	• Check homework (Unit 7, Task 3) and discuss flowchart (page 90) • CB Unit 8, Introduction (page 94) • CB Unit 8, Task 1 (pages 95–96): *Features of abstracts*	• CB Unit 8, Task 2, Ex 2.1 (pages 96–98): *Conference abstracts*
(Session 2)	• Return first drafts and make general comments • Distribute written feedback sheets • CB Unit 8, Task 2, Exs 2.2. and 2.3 (page 98): *Conference abstracts*	• Writing second drafts; must respond to comments on feedback sheets
(Session 3)	• Submitting abstract	• Conference presentation abstract deadline
(Session 4)	• Tutorials: discuss second drafts; students bring feedback sheets	• Writing second drafts

Date	Lesson content	Homework
Week 5 (Session 1)	• CB Unit 8 (page 102): *Editing your written work*	• Writing second drafts
(Session 2)	• Catch-up • Second draft peer-evaluation; concentrate on introductions and conclusions • Discuss presentations; familiarize students with assessment forms	• Complete second drafts for negotiated deadline
(Session 3)	• Tutorials and catch-up	• Presentation preparation
(Session 4)	• CB Unit 8, Task 3 (pages 99–100): *Preparing an oral presentation*	• Presentation preparation
Week 6 (Session 1)	• Course evaluation questionnaire. • Feedback to individuals about project, as appropriate	
(Session 2)	• Conference presentations: Students base their presentations on an aspect of their projects	

Introduction to the skills of extended writing and research

This unit will help students:
- learn more about extended writing and what it involves;
- find out about writing a project.

Introduction

This unit introduces students to extended writing and informs them about the projects they will work on in this book. Introduce the course by explaining that it will help students to develop practical skills for extended writing. They will also learn to carry out research in the library and online, so that they have the necessary information to tackle extended essays.

The term 'project' is used throughout the course because the main focus of the course is to complete either one or two projects/pieces of extended writing. Refer students to the Contents and Book Map pages of the Course Book (pages 3–5) for the area of focus of each unit, and to the Introduction (pages 7–8) for the aims of the Course Book and the skills it will help them to develop.

Briefly talk through the steps at the bottom of page 12 and point out that students will get the opportunity to practise each of the steps in this book.

Task 1: Critical thinking

Possible answers:
- assessing the writer's argument critically
- comparing and evaluating issues
- evaluating the credibility of the writer's sources
- detecting bias
- differentiating between main and supporting ideas
- justifying ideas, comments and analyses used by the writer

Task 2: What do students in higher education write?

2.1 Tell students to write for no more than five minutes. Quickly ask around the class for suggestions about the type of writing they might have to do at university.

Possible answers:
The following types of writing are suggested on page 12 of the Course Book.
- essays for examinations
- extended essays or projects
- reports
- theses
- dissertations
- case studies
- notes
- annotations (e.g., on handouts or photocopied originals)

If students mention any of these types of writing, or anything else that seems relevant, write them on the board.

2.2 Get students to read the boxed text on page 11 in order to compare their ideas with what is written there. Elicit any other types of writing that are mentioned in the Course Book and add them to the list on the board.

Note: The terms *thesis* and *dissertation* are used differently in different countries and even in different universities in the same country. In most universities in the UK, Hong Kong and Australia, a thesis is written for the research degree of PhD or MPhil, while a much shorter dissertation is one of the final requirements for a taught Master's degree. In many American universities, the terms are reversed, with theses written at Master's level and a doctoral dissertation at PhD level. For our purposes, the Hong Kong, UK and Australian terms for a PhD thesis and a taught Master's dissertation are used. See Bunton, D. (2002). Generic moves in PhD Thesis. In J. Flowerdew (Ed.) *Academic Discourse*. London: Pearson Education.

Task 3: Types of writing

This task is meant simply to enhance students' understanding of the types and length of writing they may have to do. It also clarifies the level of study at which the various types of writing are practised. The sample answers below are repeated as a photocopiable handout on page 23.

Possible answers:

Type of writing	Type of student	Explanation
essay for an examination	undergraduate/postgraduate	traditional 600–1,000-word text written during an exam
non-examination essay	undergraduate/postgraduate	written work submitted as part of the course requirement during term time – typically 600–6,000 words.
report	undergraduate/postgraduate	describes research
dissertation	undergraduate/postgraduate	Bachelor's level: usually 10,000–12,000 words Master's level: usually 15,000–20,000 words
thesis	postgraduate	doctorate level: this will be much longer than a dissertation
case study	undergraduate/postgraduate	an account that gives detailed information about a person, group or thing and its development over a period of time
notes	undergraduate/postgraduate	information recorded from written sources, lectures, seminars or tutorials, for later reference
annotations	undergraduate/postgraduate	comments, explanations or highlighting added to written sources or lecture handouts

Types of assessment

Explain to students that they can find out what type of assessment is used in their individual departments by checking the appropriate handbook. The Meteorology Department at the University of Reading, for example, provides an online handbook that contains information on assessment. An alternative may be to check in the relevant undergraduate or postgraduate prospectus. However, information on assessment is not consistent and is not always present.

The best way to find out about written assessment expectations is for the student to visit her/his particular university department and ask for samples of assessed written work. Emphasize that all three forms of assessment mentioned on page 13 of the Course Book are equally important – continuous, written and oral.

Explain that continuous assessment is based on how students carry out their research and organize their time and work, and on how they cooperate with fellow students and teachers, as well as on attendance and participation in class activities. Emphasize the link between written and spoken language components of any course. Explain that students are expected to put the lessons of other components of their course into practice when working on projects or written tasks. You may choose to hold a conference at the end of the course, where all students are expected to give an oral presentation (of about 10 minutes) or a poster presentation. Advice on how to prepare for a poster presentation is given in Unit 8 of the Course Book.

Task 4: Participating in a tutorial

Possible answers:
- the thesis statement
- the logical organization of ideas
- the appropriate use of academic conventions and style
- the introduction and conclusion
- the appropriate use of sources, e.g., where from, how many, currency, authority

Guided Projects 1 and 2
Go through the information on page 14 of the Course Book with students, as well as the information under the heading *Writing projects* on page 13, and answer any questions they may have. Explain that students will be able to practise one-to-one tutorials in Unit 4, but will also be having such tutorials with you at regular intervals during the course.

For students using this book for a longer 8-week or 11-week course, the written project should be regarded as practice for a second assignment. Students on a shorter, five-week course will only complete one compulsory project.

Task 5: Analyzing the task

Answers:
a) The title is framed as a question: *To what extent …?* Ask students what they understand by this.
b) Remind students that a question requires an answer. Elicit a range of answers that the question *To what extent* might produce, e.g., *a great deal, quite a lot, not much, not at all.* Explain to students that they must decide '*To what extent*' through their research and then they must explain their answer in their project, using the evidence in the sources they are given to support their argument.

Task 6: The stages of writing a project

The aim of this task is for students to discuss and cooperate in the decision-making process. Establish that writing a project is a process. Explain that there are three distinct phases involved in the process: planning, researching and writing up. Within each phase, there are also a number of stages. Task 6 involves deciding which stages occur during which phases of the process. Make sure students appreciate that certain stages can occur in more than one phase.

Before you set this task, check/explain the key terms below:

- *rough outline;*
- *establishing a clear focus;*
- *working title;*
- *sources;*
- *tutorial.*

6.1 Remind students to write out the steps in full; *not* to simply write down the letter for each step, as this provides a better reference for future use. An alternative procedure suggested by a colleague at CALS, Jonathan Smith, is to put the students in groups and give them slips of paper with the different stages of the writing process on them. They should also be given some blank pieces of paper to add any stages they may wish, an A3 sheet of paper and a gluestick. Students can then make a poster with arrows, linking lines, etc., to help visualize the writing process. Make it clear that students will probably have different views.

Possible answers:

Planning
1 j) Decide on a topic.
2 p) Check that sources are available/accessible.
3 c) Think of a working title for the project.
4 o) Make a rough outline plan of your ideas.
5 n) Work on establishing a clear focus.
6 m) Plan the contents in detail.

Researching
1 d) Search for relevant journals/ books/information in the library and on the Internet.
2 e) Write down the details of your sources.
3 l) Highlight/take notes of relevant information.
4 i) Do some reading.
5 f) Decide if you need to do more reading.

Writing up
1 k) Write the first complete draft.
2 a) Read the first draft.
3 b) Edit the draft – decide objectively whether your ideas have been expressed clearly.
4 h) Arrange a tutorial with your tutor.
5 g) Write the contents page, bibliography, title page and abstract.

The answer key above is open to discussion, and it should be presented to students in this way.

6.2 Arrange the class in pairs or groups to discuss the possible phases and stages in the answer key. Ask students if there are any stages that they think are missing from the phases. Finally, ask how the third, *writing up* phase would continue, i.e., *write second draft; read draft; edit,* etc. (the process should be repeated as necessary).

Learner independence: Appendix 2
The aims of the self-evaluation task in Appendix 2, Course Book pages 119–120, are:
- to raise students' awareness of the skills necessary for extended writing and oral presentations;
- to get students to consider which aspects of these skills they need to develop further.

An important aim of this course is to encourage learner independence. One aspect of this independence is students' ability to assess themselves realistically, in order to recognize the particular skills they need to develop. Appendix 2 has a checklist of the skills students will work on during this course. Ask them to fill in the checklist for homework (do the first point in class as an example), then discuss it briefly in the following lesson, i.e., ask students which aspects they feel they can deal with, and which ones they need to concentrate on.

Task 7: Starting Project 1

The questions on page 17 of the Course Book are intended to provide students with a framework for getting them started on their first project, but may also be the basis for a framework for a second project (if appropriate). Please point out this fact to students who are on a longer course, and refer to it again when they begin their second project.

7.1 Get the students to check their ideas from Task 5. Then tell the students to read the questions in the 'Introduction' section on page 17.

7.2 In small groups, students should briefly discuss their responses. Repeat this process with the 'Main body' and 'Conclusion' sections. At the end of each of the three stages (about five minutes of group discussion), it would be a good idea to have a brief whole-class discussion so that the groups can share ideas.

Students may have already encountered the idea of 'brainstorming' in *English for academic study: Writing*. If not, it would be a good idea to demonstrate the technique using a simple topic, e.g., 'The benefits of attending a pre-sessional course'. This is also an opportunity to demonstrate writing in note form – get students to identify examples of note form after you've completed your 'brainstorm' on the board. When the majority of students have written down their ideas in the boxes on page 18, elicit a few examples for each section.

Explain to students that they may find some of their ideas have been written about in more detail in the sources that they will meet when they begin Unit 2. They may change their minds about which are the most relevant ideas as a result of reading the sources, and they will probably come across other ideas that they had not thought of.

Unit summary

You may want the students to complete the unit summaries in class or in their own time. If they complete them out of class, make sure you get some feedback during class time.

You may wish to set up some of the activities, either to clarify what to do, or to help get students thinking about the topics.

Some of the items can be done individually and others are best done in pairs or groups. When working outside the classroom, encourage students to find the time to meet with others and complete any pair or group activities.

1   **Answers:**
   a) develop
   b) provide
   c) dispute
   d) display

4   Possible answers:

a) decide on a topic / check that sources are available/accessible / think of a working title for the project / work on establishing a clear focus / plan the contents in detail

b) search for relevant information / write down details of sources / highlight or take notes of relevant information / do some reading / decide if you need to do more reading

c) write the first complete draft / read the first draft / edit the first draft / arrange a tutorial with your tutor / write the contents page, bibliography, title page and abstract

Web resources

CUNY WriteSite: Writing a project
The 'stages of writing' section gives ideas and tips on ways of approaching the different stages of the writing process, in relation to extended writing.
http://writesite.cuny.edu/projects/index.html

UNESCO: Education for Sustainable Development
The 'news' and 'archives' sections provide links to and give brief summaries of projects and campaigns around the world that are promoting sustainable development in urban areas.
http://portal.unesco.org/education/en/ev.php-
URL_ID=32524&URL_DO=DO_TOPIC&URL_SECTION=201.html

Additional online activities

Additional interactive activities to accompany this unit can be found online, at
www.english acacdemicstudy.com

Photocopiable handout

Types of writing

Type of writing	Type of student	Explanation
essay for an examination	undergraduate/ postgraduate	traditional 600–1,000-word text written during an exam
non-examination essay	undergraduate/ postgraduate	written work submitted as part of the course requirement during term time – typically 600–6,000 words
report	undergraduate/ postgraduate	describes research
dissertation	undergraduate/ postgraduate	Bachelor's level: usually 10,000–12,000 words Master's level: usually 15,000–20,000 words
thesis	postgraduate	doctorate level: this will be much longer than a dissertation
case study	undergraduate/ postgraduate	an account that gives detailed information about a person, group or thing and its development over a period of time
notes	undergraduate/ postgraduate	information recorded from written sources, lectures, seminars or tutorials, for later reference
annotations	undergraduate/ postgraduate	comments, explanations or highlighting added to written sources or lecture handouts

Photocopiable

Using evidence to support your ideas

This unit will help students:
- discuss the importance of providing evidence in academic writing;
- learn different methods of incorporating sources;
- practise summarizing information.

Go over the Introduction carefully with the students. Emphasize that using and acknowledging sources of information and ideas adds weight to academic argument.

Reading list
The printed sources in the reading list are in Appendix 4 of the Course Book (pages 123–158). Students should be reminded that not all of the information in the sources is relevant; some will be more useful than the rest. Students have to read selectively to choose the most relevant information to help them write their projects.

Task 1: Selective reading

1.1 After a few minutes, elicit answers from pairs of students.

Possible answers:
a) To find information to help write the project.
b) Selectively – students will have to decide which information appears to be most useful and relevant *as they are reading*. They may bring up the idea of skimming for general content, or scanning for specific information.
c) Underline key points, make notes in the margin of the text or make notes on separate paper.

Task 2: Incorporating evidence into academic work

2.1 Answer:
The best answer is **b)**. The writer enumerates the increase (10 per cent) and reports the source and the date – therefore the reader will have more *confidence* in the information. Evidence for the writer's ideas is provided by referencing expert views (*expertise*) in the field. These experts have undoubtedly carried out detailed practical or theoretical research.

2.2 Answers:

a) Any discussion of financial markets must begin with a <u>definition</u> of what they are: "<u>A financial market is the place or mechanism whereby financial assets are exchanged and prices of these assets are set</u>" (Campbell, 2003, p. 47).
b) According to Wang (2001) <u>education is the key aspect underlying the successful economic development in a society</u>.
c) Djabri states that <u>operations research is the application of the methods of science to complex problems</u> (Djabri, 2005).
d) As Sloman (2006) has demonstrated, <u>there are two main methods of measuring unemployment.</u>
e) <u>This antibiotic has an immediate effect on the illness</u> (Braine, 2007).

Task 3: Referencing

3.1 References to be highlighted are given in the first column of the table below.

3.2 Make sure that students understand the difference between a *direct* and an *indirect* reference. These examples of ways of incorporating references are an introduction to the tasks that follow.

3.1/3.3 Answers:

Name and date	Direct/indirect reference	Idea expressed
O'Riordan, 1976	indirect	E
John Muir (quoted in Pepper, 1984)	direct (This is an example of the writer quoting a source that has been quoted in a previous work.)	D
Ronald Inglehart (1977)	direct	C
Maslow (1970)	direct	A
Cotgrove & Duff, 1980	indirect	F
Downs, 1972	indirect	B

Students may have been introduced to identifying information in texts and summarizing ideas in *English for academic study: Writing*. Emphasize that writing a project gives them the opportunity to put into practice the skills they are being taught in other components of their course. Evidence of appropriate referencing is expected in their projects, and is essential in academic writing.

Task 4: Purposeful reading

As a homework task, get students to transfer two of the definitions they find in the sources to a table, such as the one below. You may wish to direct students in particular to the source in Appendix 4.4, 'Sustainability' by W. M. Adams.

Definition	Author	Date	Title	Page number	Source of publication
Sustainable development is 'development that meets the needs of the present without compromising the ability of future generations to meet their own needs' (Bruntland, 1987, p. 43).	Adams, W.M. in P. Cloke et al. (Eds.)	1999	Sustainability in *Introducing human geographies*	pp. 125–130	London: Arnold

Summarizing information from texts

Summarizing may have been covered in other components of the students' course; however, it is worth going over the points made here to refresh their memory. The idea of the N.O.W. approach, on page 28 of the Course Book, is that students summarize from their notes, but you must remind them to always make a note of the source of the resulting summary.

The source still has to be acknowledged, even if students write the summary in their own words – the ideas are the 'intellectual property' of the original writer.

Students usually find the task of summarizing information – trying to express a set of ideas in their own words – extremely challenging. At times, it can be difficult to convince them that incorporating information from texts into their own work without referencing is not academically acceptable. The aim of this section is to take the students through some steps to make summarizing easier, and to raise their awareness of the dangers of plagiarism.

Two key factors should be emphasized throughout.
- Students should have a purpose when they summarize. For example, presenting a writer's viewpoint, which they may support or disagree with.
- Students need to interact with the text in some way in order to fully comprehend it, i.e., think carefully about the meaning. Emphasize that it is not useful to attempt to summarize if they have not fully understood the text. For this reason, it can be very useful to have students verbalize the ideas first, explaining the content of what they have read before they actually write.

Task 5: Features of a summary

5.2   The aim of this task is to raise awareness and generate discussion.

Answers:
a   This is not necessary, unless there is a set of steps or a process that logically needs to have the same order as the original.
b   No. The point of the summary is to choose what is relevant for the reader's purpose.
c   No. It is important to emphasize that specialist vocabulary is essential and cannot be changed. Clarify that a summary should be in the students' own words, but not to the extent that they use inappropriate vocabulary in order to avoid the words in the text. Point out here that actually telling someone their ideas can be helpful; students will thus avoid using too much of the same vocabulary.
d   Yes. This will probably occur naturally if students are writing from their notes.
e   Yes. Part of the skill of summarizing is emphasizing the important points (but without directly saying *I think this is important*).
f   Definitely not within the summary itself. However, the student may be required to comment on the content of the summary as part of a task.

Task 6: Stages in writing a summary or paraphrase

The aim of this task is to encourage good summarizing practice. Tell students to read through the stages individually. Ultimately, the stages should be analyzed as a group or whole-class activity. You might like to put the text to be summarized on an OHT for students to discuss first, before referring them to the sample summary in their books (see page 31 of this book). It is useful for them to work through the process together, as a model for future reference. Get students to explain the four stages of summary writing in their own words.

Taking notes: Appendix 3
You may like to refer students to Appendix 3 (Course Book pages 121–122) at this stage, for some advice on taking notes. Suggested answers to the tasks in Appendix 3 appear below.

Task 1: Taking notes when listening or reading

Possible answers:

Listening	Reading
You only hear it once, cannot rewind.	You can read it again and again.
You are trying to do three things at once: listen, understand and write.	You have time first to read, understand and then take notes.
stressful – time restriction	no time restriction
There is no way to check accuracy/details.	You can check details in original source.
A lecturer will pick out the important points.	You need to pick out the important points.

Task 3: Note-taking strategies

Possible answers:
- Look at your notes several days later and check that you can still understand them (if you can't, you need to rethink your note-taking strategy).
- Look at your notes several days later and highlight the main points.
- Look at your notes and explain the content to someone else (this will help to enhance your own understanding of the notes).

Task 7: Practice summary 1

The aim of this task and Task 8 is to encourage students to extract information selectively and write summaries based on their own notes rather than directly from a text. Point out that the amount of relevant material extracted from the texts on both occasions is relatively small. The purpose of taking notes in the first place determines the type of notes that are taken.

7.2   Below are some guidelines, but obviously there may be variations – key points are underlined. This model answer is repeated as a photocopiable handout on page 32.

Model answer:

The making of modern Japan
Modern Japan is a nation of contradictions. Economically powerful and prosperous, its future economic prosperity depends on continued access to reliable sources of external raw materials and stable markets. Militarily constrained because of its U.S.-created constitution, Japan relies on U.S. military strength and the benign intention of others to maintain its security. Pro-Western and modern in its cultural outlook, it reveres old Japanese traditions and customs. The contradictions that exist in Japan – and influence its perceptions of itself and the world – are a product of Japan's historical experiences.

From a global perspective, Japan is a unique nation. With a population half that of the United States and a gross national product 40 percent the size of the United States, Japan must import large percentages of almost every raw material that modern industrialized societies need. Since Japan's evolution to an industrial power did not begin until the late nineteenth century, and since it had no scientific technical tradition, the strides it took to transform itself into a relatively modern industrial state by the beginning of the twentieth century were truly amazing.

Notes

Japan – into mod. ind. society despite contradictions
- late industrialization/very fast
- no scientific tradition
- dependency on raw materials from outside

Summary

Japan's rise to economic success is based on contradictions. It needs to import huge amounts of raw materials to support its industry. Its economic development in the nineteenth century is remarkable, especially considering its lack of scientific tradition.

Task 8: Practice summary 2

Get students to predict possible causes of the decline of animal species before they read the text, e.g., pollution, climate change, human activity.

8.2 Model answer:

Notes
Causes of decline:
- under-crowding
- leading to low population density
- 'Allee effects'
- e.g., pigeon pop. of 18c

Summary
One possible reason for the decline of animal species is under-crowding, known as the Allee effect. This happens, against apparent logic, when a population that may have been extremely well populated begins to fall, and continues to do so to the extent of being in danger of extinction.

Task 9: Practice summary 3

For this final summarizing task, get students to access the appropriate texts from the list of references given on page 21. Tell students to use the N.O.W. approach to carry out their summaries, as they did for Tasks 7 and 8.

Unit summary

3   Answers:

It is important that any claim, opinion or generalization made in an essay is supported by evidence. You need to show proof that what you are saying is correct. To incorporate evidence into your writing, you can paraphrase a specific idea from the writer in your own words or you can summarize the content of a text (write a shorter version which concentrates on the main information). Occasionally, you might want to use direct quotations (the writer's exact words). When you use other people's ideas, you must acknowledge them. This means referring to them both within the text and in a bibliography at the end of the text.

4   Possible answers:

   a)   make sure I understand the text I am summarizing / decide on a clear purpose for the summary / make notes as I read the text / highlight or underline key points in the text / use my own words to express ideas

b) summarize a text I don't understand properly / use the writer's exact words or make all the same points in the same order as the writer without acknowledgement (plagiarize)

Web resources

UEfAP: Academic writing: Reporting
This site contains a step-by-step guide to academic writing. In the 'Reporting' section, there is useful information on how to paraphrase and how to write a summary or synthesis. You will also find practice summary writing exercises with model answers.
http://www.uefap.com/writing/writfram.htm

Language and learning online: Why do we reference?
These pages from the Monash University website give more detailed information about referencing conventions and why it is important to refer to the sources we use in academic writing.
http://www.monash.edu.au/lls/llonline/writing/general/reference/index.xml

Additional online activities

Additional interactive activities to accompany this unit can be found online, at www.englishforacademicstudy.com.

Environmental problems and management

Interest in the environment is not a recent phenomenon; the environment has always affected the growth and development of humankind, as a source of materials as well as a refuge for the human spirit. The recent interest in protecting the environment is a reflection of both the demand of society for a better quality of life, which may include using the environment as a haven, as well as the need to replenish sources. The difference between the present day and the pre-1960s era is the extent to which concern for the environment has become important; there is much greater interest …

Source: Jordan, A. & O'Riordan, T. (1999). Environmental problems and management. In P. Cloke, P. Crang & M. Goodwin (Eds.), Introducing human geographies (pp. 133-140). London: Arnold.

The making of modern Japan

Modern Japan is a nation of contradictions. Economically powerful and prosperous, its future economic prosperity depends on continued access to reliable sources of external raw materials and stable markets. Militarily constrained because of its U.S.-created constitution, Japan relies on U.S. military strength and the benign intention of others to maintain its security. Pro-Western and modern in its cultural outlook, it reveres old Japanese traditions and customs. The contradictions that exist in Japan – and influence its perceptions of itself and the world – are a product of Japan's historical experiences.

From a global perspective, Japan is a unique nation. With a population half that of the United States and a gross national product 40 percent the size of the United States, Japan must import large percentages of almost every raw material that modern industrialized societies need. Since Japan's evolution to an industrial power did not begin until the late nineteenth century, and since it had no scientific technical tradition, the strides it took to transform itself into a relatively modern industrial state by the beginning of the twentieth century were truly amazing.

Notes
Japan – into mod. ind. society despite contradictions
- late industrialization/very fast
- no scientific tradition
- dependency on raw materials from outside

Summary
Japan's rise to economic success is based on contradictions. It needs to import huge amounts of raw materials to support its industry. Its economic development in the nineteenth century is remarkable, especially considering its lack of scientific tradition.

3 Structuring your project and finding information

This unit will help students:
- look at how a project is structured;
- learn to identify evaluative writing;
- practise academic referencing;
- practise selecting information from websites.

Task 1: The structure of projects

The aim of this section is to familiarize students with a typical first project. The length, features and format of the sample project *To what extent should insider dealing be regulated, and how can this be done effectively?* in Appendix 1 (Course Book pages 109–118) make it a reasonable approximation of what students should be aiming for. The project was completed by a pre-sessional student and was chosen because it is about a fairly accessible topic, but contains some useful examples of academic style and conventions (e.g., quotations and a bibliography). It is also generally well organized, with an introduction, a main body and a conclusion.

This project makes use of a number of sources, and a range of arguments are used to give a balanced viewpoint. Students should be encouraged to identify the various opinions being expressed and to identify areas where the writer (Mansoor Alhagbani) appears to express his own opinion, for example, in the conclusion.

Clearly, in this project, the student has attempted to express ideas in his own words and to support the points he makes with reference to sources. Again, this can be pointed out to students and it should be explained that work on avoiding plagiarism is carried out in later units of the Course Book.

There is also a thesis statement in the introduction, namely that "all forms of insider dealing should be regulated … through a proactive approach". This is developed further in the conclusion by the writer suggesting that "combating it [insider trading] can be achieved by preventing it".

The extent to which you want to address the three above points at this stage, if at all, will depend very much on the level of the students in the group, as well as on time constraints. However, they are points that must be emphasized at some stage of the course.

1.1 This is intended purely as a familiarization task, so that students have a clear idea of typical components of the project they are expected to write. Discuss the parts of an academic text, as listed in the Course Book, before students look through the project.

1.2 Allow students some time to look through the project and label the various parts. Several of the sections, e.g., the introduction, abstract and bibliography, are already appropriately headed, but others, such as quotations or references in the text, do have to be identified.

It would be a good idea to put the class into groups of three or four students and then circulate and confirm that every student has labelled the various sections of the project appropriately.

How to write an evaluative project

It is worthwhile to point out the importance of students being evaluative or critical in their writing from the beginning. They should establish a clear focus and develop a strong thesis for their project. The writer's 'position' should be a thread that runs through the whole essay, giving it cohesion and coherence. The example of the plan for the project on the restructuring of the Korean banking system illustrates this very clearly.

1.4   It is recommended that you make an OHT of the flow chart on page 35 of the Course Book, and display it for general discussion. Go through the model in detail, emphasizing the role that critical reading plays throughout the writing of a project.

Task 2: Descriptive and evaluative writing

The purpose of this task is to help students identify the different features of descriptive and evaluative writing. Each of the four paragraphs contains elements of both descriptive and evaluative writing, and this should be pointed out. However, certain paragraphs are predominantly evaluative, e.g., paragraph 4 (which in fact forms the conclusion of the full article).

Answers:

Paragraph	Mainly descriptive	Evaluative comments
1	✓	✓
2		✓
3	✓	✓
4		✓

2.2   After completing the table, students should be encouraged to identify (by underlining) examples of evaluative text. Explain that the italicized text below is evaluative because it expresses an opinion or attitude about the facts that are given in the rest of the text. The italicized examples mostly illustrate caution on the part of the writer (which is often typical of academic style). This is particularly true of paragraphs 1 and 4. An extension of this exercise would be to ask students to express the evaluative examples in their own words.

Answers:
Examples of evaluative writing are identified in italics below.

Paragraph 1
… Because of the new investment opportunities they provide and because their experiences *may offer* lessons for less developed economies …

Paragraph 2
… These numbers *make it clear that* external trade has been *an important element* in the development of these economies.

Paragraph 3
Commercial banks *also played a critical role, because they were the major source* of private savings.

Paragraph 4
… The figures *seem to reflect* the emphases of the past development policies. "The financial system *was rather the accommodator of this real economic performance than its instigator*," wrote one economist after examining the role of the financial sector in economic development experiences of these economies (Patrick, 1994). Recent banking sector developments in Korea and, to a lesser extent, Taiwan *point to the negative side-effects that government direction of credit to preferred industries can have in the long run*. Singapore's experience *seems to suggest* that a government *could implement* industrial development policies without directing the credit decisions of the commercial banking sector. Finally, Hong Kong's case *seems to illustrate that* an active industrial policy *may not be essential* for rapid economic development.

Task 3: Reading for a specific purpose

Reading for a purpose is a key concept and this section reinforces the work done in *English for academic study: Reading* and *English for academic study: Writing*.

Task 4: Choosing sources

The purpose of this task is to get students to think about the selection of texts for their work. For this project, all the texts are chosen for them, but for the second project on this course (if students are doing the longer course), and indeed for future written projects, they will need to find sources for themselves. Work through the fifth text in Appendix 4, Sustainable urban livelihoods, following the example, then get students to complete the table for three more sources in Appendix 4.

Possible answers:

TEXT	Thisdell, D. (1993). Can L.A. kick the car habit? *New Scientist, 138* (1877), 24–29.
Why it was chosen	• published in *New Scientist*, a reputable, science-oriented popular magazine • deals directly with problems to do with urbanization, e.g., transport congestion and pollution, focusing on Los Angeles • examines the challenges in urban planning • examines problems and solutions, i.e., discursive*
TEXT	Chaffey, J. (1994). The challenge of urbanisation. In M. Naish & S. Warn (Eds.), *Core geography* (pp. 138–146). London: Longman.
Why it was chosen	• looks specifically at housing, which is another key issue in urban problems, focusing on Hong Kong • is a case study and therefore a primary source • contains figures and tables with statistical data relating to urban planning
TEXT	Adams, W.M. (1999). Sustainability. In P. Cloke, P. Crang & M. Goodwin (Eds.), *Introducing human geographies* (pp. 125–130). London: Arnold.
Why it was chosen	• fairly recent publication (1999) from a reputable publisher • provides a definition of sustainability in detail with reference to different fields, e.g., economics, geography and science • refers to the Brundtland Report – a key document in defining sustainable development
TEXT	Elliot, J.A. (1999). *An introduction to sustainable development*. London: Routledge.
Why it was chosen	• examines the effect of population growth on essential services, e.g., sanitation, water supply • takes a more global view than the other sources of the growth of cities, e.g., see Figure 5.3 Economic-environmental typology of cities • raises awareness of differences between the Brown Agenda and the Green Agenda
TEXT	Newman, P. (1999). Transport: reducing automobile dependence. In D. Satterthwaite (Ed.), *The Earthscan reader in sustainable cities* (pp. 67–92). London: Earthscan Publications.
Why it was chosen	• fairly recent article (1999), originally published by a reputable publisher, Earthscan Publications • provides case studies of attempts to deal with transport issues • provides an evaluation of solutions to the problem of automobile dependency (see section 'Key Policy Conclusions')

* You might like to point out to students that this is a good example of evaluative writing, as a follow-up to Task 2.

Task 5: Finding information

Finding information in textbooks

Students will probably already have had a library introduction at some point. Increasingly, students tend to use web-based sources for their work, and avoid using the library. However, their future departments will expect them to be fully familiar with how to use the library facilities, and the location of journals and books related to their subject area.

5.1 Filling in the tables requires students to think about their selection of sources, which is one aspect of developing critical thinking. This exercise should be completed as a homework task. Students can feed back (Exercise 5.2) in class.

Finding information in journals

Encourage students to find out which journals are favoured by their departments. Articles can be useful as the starting point for research, and abstracts are invaluable in ascertaining if an article is relevant to a student's purpose.

Making use of abstracts

Work on abstracts is covered in more detail in Units 4 and 8. You could refer students to Task 4 in Unit 4 at this point, if appropriate to their needs.

Task 6: Analyzing websites

For this task, you will need to book the computer laboratory or class-in-a-box. You will need to go over the criteria for website evaluation with students. Emphasize the importance of using only reliable websites, e.g., if an author/organization cannot be identified, or if there is no date, then there is no way of knowing whether the information is accurate.

Task 7: Acknowledging your sources

This section extends the work on referencing that students did in Unit 2. Experience shows that even when students feel they have control of the conventions of referencing, they make mistakes in bibliographies and when referencing within a text.

Elicit what students already know about referencing. Ask students how and why we reference sources. (They should be able to draw on work done in Unit 2 for this.)

7.1 For answers, see Course Book page 45.

7.2 As consolidation, you could put samples of students' work with incorrect referencing on an OHT, and ask the students to correct the mistakes.

Task 9: When to avoid using online sources

There are a range of possible reasons for not using websites that do not have the name of the author or an organization. Elicit ideas from the students before you show them the list below.

- The academic credentials of the writer are unknown.
- The information or ideas may be out of date.
- The information or ideas may be untrue or unreliable.
- It is inconvenient to have to check the validity of the information.
- Without credentials you cannot quote or paraphrase the information.

Task 10: Writing a bibliography

10.1 Answers:

a)	title of article	4
b)	name of publisher	10
c)	date of publication	3
d)	author's surname	1
e)	title of book	8
f)	editor's surname	5
g)	place of publication	9
h)	author's initials	2
i)	other editors	6
j)	shows book is a collection of articles (or chapters)	7

10.2 Answers:

Adams, W.M. (1999). Sustainability. In P. Cloke, P. Crang & M. Goodwin (Eds.), *Introducing human geographies*. (pp. 125–130). London: Arnold.

Bilham-Boult, A., Blades, H., Hancock, J., Keeling, W. & Ridout, M. (1999). *People, places and themes*. Oxford: Heinemann.

Harch, E. (2003). Africa Recovery. Retrieved May 18, 2004, from http://www.africarecovery.org

Newman, P. (1999). Transport: reducing automobile dependence. In D. Satterwaite, (Ed.), *The Earthscan reader in sustainable cities* (pp. 67–92). London: Earthscan Publications.

Note: The detailed model bibliographical entries in Appendix 5 ('Compiling a bibliography', Course Book pages 159–160) are very useful for reference, until students get used to laying out bibliographies themselves.

Web resources

The UVic writer's guide: acknowledging your sources
The 'Acknowledging your sources' section of the University of Victoria guide to academic writing looks at primary and secondary sources and how to refer to them in your writing. The sub-section on bibliographies helps you to understand how bibliographies are organized, and the sections on quotations and citations give very detailed information about how to quote from and cite different types of text.
http://web.uvic.ca/wguide/Pages/MasterToc.html#Sources

A student's guide to www research
A guide from St Louis University on how to find information online. It covers many areas, including how to assess whether a site is suitable for academic use and how to use find information using search engines.
http://www.slu.edu/colleges/AS/ENG/cai/research/

Additional online activities

Additional interactive activities to accompany this unit can be found online, at www.englishforacademicstudy.com.

Developing your project

This unit will help students:
- find out how to make the best use of the tutorial system;
- learn about plagiarism and how to avoid it;
- learn about the features of abstracts and their purpose.

The tutorial system is fully described in the Course Book, but it is worth going through this as a whole-class activity.

Task 1: Preparing for tutorials

The format of any feedback sheet that you may already use for drafts of the students' work should be discussed. On the back of the sheet used at the University of Reading, there is a breakdown (A–D) of each component of the project that should be assessed and a set of descriptors explaining the particular grade of each component (see pages 87–88 of this book). Assessment sheets should be carefully explained to students. This is probably best done with the whole class in the first instance and then with individuals in one-to-one tutorials.

Content

A major problem with the projects produced by pre-sessional students is that they tend to be over-descriptive. There is very little discussion involved. One way to encourage comments is to get students to answer questions about the topic of their project.

Example procedure:

- Write the title of the project on the board:
  To what extent can the problems of urbanization be met by a policy of sustainable development?
- Underline the phrase *To what extent*.
- Draw a line on the board and label it with the phrases *not at all* and *completely* at appropriate ends of the continuum.
- Write the phrases: *quite a lot*; *to a certain extent*; *a bit*; *to a great extent* in random order. Students should label the diagram as below.

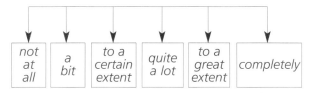

| not at all | a bit | to a certain extent | quite a lot | to a great extent | completely |

- Get students to choose one of these phrases in order to answer the question.
- When students have made their choice about the 'extent', get them to answer the question *Why?*
- Tell students to write down the term *because* and, below it, write between three and five reasons taken from the evidence they have been reading as research.
  Example: Because of the efforts made by international organizations, such as Greenpeace, to encourage sustainable development.
- As an extension, you could write the word *however* and ask students to write alternatives to the points they have written under *because*. The end result might look something like the example below.

because:
- *of the efforts made by international organizations, such as Greenpeace, to encourage sustainable development.*

however:
- *sustainable development policies are very expensive to introduce, especially in LEDCs.*

Organization

A project should be organized in such a way that the main ideas are clear and linked to the introduction and conclusion. The text should be coherent, i.e., there should be a logical development of ideas. The text should also be cohesive, i.e., the ideas in the text should be connected linguistically through the use of appropriate linking words, anaphoric and cataphoric referents, etc.

Language

Students should be issued with error correction codes. This helps them to identify the types of errors they have made and is a step towards independent error correction. Error correction codes tend to work most efficiently with higher-level students and are a useful instrument to encourage independent editing. However, it is important to point students in the right direction for any remedial language work needed. This can be achieved both through the error correction sheet and through written comments on the feedback sheet about certain language issues they might address (see the example in the Course Book).

Presentation of work

This has become less of a problem as students now submit their work electronically. However, they need to be given advice about such things as which fonts to use for letter size, as well as style, headings and subheadings, bullets and numbering, pagination, the incorporation of tables and figures, and the incorporation of footnotes.

Use of sources

Students must be convinced that the use of sources is an essential requirement of academic writing. Referencing/citing and bibliographies are dealt with in Units 2 and 3 as well as this unit. Students should be encouraged to follow the appropriate academic conventions appropriately and consistently.

Task 2: Quotations, paraphrases and plagiarism

The aim of this task is to get students to identify examples of quotes and paraphrases and also to recognize where plagiarism has occurred.

Answers:

	Quotation or paraphrase	Plagiarism	Comment
1	paraphrase	no	The original idea is restated in the student's own words and correctly referenced.
2	quotation	yes	The words are lifted directly from the original Papp article without any attempt to either quote or cite the original source.
3	paraphrase	yes	The ideas of the original are maintained without acknowledgement, although the wording is completely different.
4	paraphrase	yes	This is plagiarism, even though the wording is completely different except 'revolutionary perspective'. The original source must be acknowledged and the lifted words enclosed within quotation marks. Emphasize to students that citing sources adds 'academic weight' to their argument.
5	quotation	no	Point out to students that quotes of three lines or more should form a separate paragraph and should be indented as demonstrated.
6	paraphrase	yes	Here, the student has lifted key phrases from the original to weave into the text without acknowledging the source.
7	quotation	no	This is a good example of the use of a very 'quotable' phrase in order to add weight to the point the student is making.

Task 3: Avoiding plagiarism

The aim of this task is to reinforce awareness of plagiarism. Each 'reason' for plagiarizing could be discussed, initially by the students in pairs and then as a whole class. There will be a variety of responses.

3.2 **Possible answers:**

a) Lack of awareness of rules:
   It is not acceptable under any circumstances.

b) Lack of familiarity with how to reference:
   You need to learn how to use references in order to write in an academic field.

c) Lack of time:
   Time management is essential when working on essays.

d) Level of difficulty of reference text:
   It is better to work from what you have read and understood than simply copy.

e) Inability to express ideas better:
   It is not expected that you write with the same level of sophistication as that in published material. Your tutor would prefer that ideas are expressed in your own words; this shows that you have more fully understood the concepts involved.

f) Different cultural experience:
   In the UK educational system, you are expected to show evidence of having thought about ideas and information rather than simply repeating them without thought.

Task 4: Working with abstracts

4.1/4.2 Get students to number various features in the margin of their book (in pencil). Encourage discussion about their findings.

Answers:

Abstract A
a) a general statement
d) an investigation into a particular topic
i) a thesis statement
c) the aims of the project

Abstract B
a) a general statement
d) and **e)** an investigation and the implementation in a real-world situation
g) details of the research carried out by the writer
h) what the results of the research suggest

4.3 **Answers:**

Abstract C
i) a thesis statement (*This project describes … It also discusses … This project describes the main achievements…*)
b) essential background information

c) the aims of the project (**b**, **c** and **i** are very closely linked in concept)

e) the implementation of the investigation in a real-world situation (*the government changing the labour laws...*)

Abstract D

b) essential background information (*Banking has developed ... However, only three banks are making a profit in the credit card market*)

a) a general statement (*It is very important ... an understanding of the credit card system used in the West*).

i) a thesis statement (*This paper will begin ... Secondly ... Finally ... their credit card business is discussed*)

4.5 This task gives students an opportunity to assess the appropriacy of project titles.

Possible answers:

Abstract	Possible title
A	*The potential provided by computer-based testing*
B	*Standardizing teaching observation practice*
C	*The development of China's security markets*
D	*The impact of the introduction of credit cards on Taiwanese banking*
E	*To what extent is risk management effective in financial institutions?*

Unit summary

1   Answers:

a) F

b) F

c) T

d) F

e) T

3   Answers:

a) theft

b) ideas

c) students' own answers

d) it could damage your academic career or stop you getting a job

e) no

f) use quotations / give references

4   Possible answers:

a) a sort of summary / a summary of the content of a text

b) they give an overall idea of what an article is about / they help you decide if an article is relevant / they clarify the purpose or aims of an article / they help you quickly access more than one article

c) a general statement / essential background information / the aims of the article / an investigation / the implementation of the investigation in a real-world situation / how the text is organized / details of the research carried out by the writer / what the results of the research suggest / a thesis statement / a definition

Web resources

The Owl at Purdue: avoiding plagiarism
The Owl is an American online writing lab for academic writers. This section explains what plagiarism is and how to avoid it.
http://owl.english.purdue.edu/owl/resource/589/01

How to write an abstract
This short article gives information about writing an abstract and provides a checklist of things to include.
http://www.ece.cmu.edu/~koopman/essays/abstract.html

Additional online activities

Additional interactive activities to accompany this unit can be found online, at www.englishforacademicstudy.com.

Developing a focus

This unit will help students:
- learn how to choose a topic;
- practise narrowing down the topic to establish a focus;
- come up with a working title;
- consolidate some of the skills they have been developing while completing Project 1.

The aim of this unit is to get students started on their projects. They should be encouraged to start looking for sources at an early stage. Check that students are familiar with the library system for cataloguing sources, such as electronic abstracts. One of the biggest problems faced by students is choosing a suitable topic. Some students will lack academic experience or will have had a very different academic background.

Finding a suitable topic therefore can be problematic. Some students may choose a topic that is far too general, such as 'global warming'. Students lacking confidence tend to do this because sources are easy to find. But the resulting problem is twofold: the information students find is often not from a suitably academic genre, and also there is such an extensive range of sources about the topic (e.g., about global warming), that students waste unnecessary time deciding which to use. Other students choose very specialized topics (this is particularly so in the case of postgraduate students), which may be unrealistic.

The important message to impress on students is that their main interest should be to perfect the *process* of completing a project. This involves: choosing a suitable topic; carrying out appropriate theoretical research; making notes; organizing ideas; writing a first draft; editing work; making use of tutorials; redrafting work in response to the advice and written comments of the project tutor, and so on. The content of the project is important, but not as important as mastering the mechanics of project writing.

Note: If lists of essay titles/topics are available from students' future academic departments, they may be useful in helping students to decide on an appropriate topic.

Task 1: Choosing a topic for your extended essay

Get students to do this individually and then discuss their lists in pairs.

Possible answers:

a)	Decide how practical it is to work on this topic.	4
b)	Find something in your subject area you are interested in.	1
c)	Summarize your project idea in one sentence.	7
d)	Decide how much you already know about the topic.	3
e)	Talk about your ideas.	5
f)	Think about a possible working title.	6
g)	Look for sources.	2
h)	Make a plan.	8

In numerical order:

1   Find something in your subject area you are interested in. (b)
2   Look for sources. (g)
3   Decide how much you already know about the topic. (d)
4   Decide how practical it is to work on this topic. (a)
5   Talk about your ideas. (e)
6   Think about a possible working title. (f)
7   Summarize your project idea in one sentence. (c)
8   Make a plan. (h)

Explain to students that there is no absolutely correct order. Ask them what a 'working title' is (*a title in the developmental stage of writing a project*).

Point out that a more specific title will probably emerge before the final version of the project is completed. Work related to finding a focus and developing more specific titles is an important part of this unit.

Task 2: Developing a topic

Explain to students that developing a specific focus will help them to choose a suitable topic title and will facilitate their search for appropriate sources. This is especially true if they are using a search engine, such as Google, or a university library search facility (such as the *Unicorn* facility at the University of Reading).

Answers:

Most general ⇒	⇐ General/Specific ⇒	⇐ Most specific
e, g	b, d, f, h	a, c

There is room for discussion with this key, e.g., **f** could be considered 'most specific'.

As a whole-class activity, get students to explain why each title belongs in each column.

Task 3: Establishing a focus

3.1 It would be best to arrange the students initially in groups or pairs. They should attempt to form questions together. Then get one group of students to present their questions and ask for further suggestions from the rest of the class. The questions below could be distributed to students for them to compare with their own (as a checklist and a basis for discussion).

Example questions for 'The education system in Argentina':
What problems exist in the Argentinean education system?
Which countries have a similar education system to Argentina?
How can the Argentinean education system be improved?

3.2 This task again lends itself to pair or groupwork and could be carried out in the same way as Ex 3.1. The sample answers below are reproduced as a photocopiable handout on page 51.

Possible answers:
Problems in the Chinese economy
What is the chief economic problem facing China?
What effects is this problem having?
Who is causing the economic problems in China?
How serious are China's economic problems?

The economy of Taiwan
How stable is the Taiwanese economy?
What drives the Taiwanese economy?

Cybernetics
(Definition: *a branch of science which involves studying the way electronic machines and human brains work, and developing machines that do things or think rather like people.* (Collins Cobuild 2001 English Dictionary).)
What is cybernetics?
How important is the work carried out in this field?
Who are the stakeholders in the area of cybernetics?

The United Nations
What is the role of the United Nations?
How effective is the United Nations?
Which area of the United Nations' work has been the most successful?

Genetically modified (GM) food
How safe is GM food?
Why is food being genetically modified?
How is food genetically modified?

Deforestation in Nepal
What has caused deforestation in Nepal?
What have been the effects of deforestation?
How is the problem of deforestation being solved?

Future developments in human health
Which areas of human health will be dealt with in future?
What developments will occur?
How will developments in human health change?
Will developments in human health add to longevity?

Task 4: Establishing a working title

The aim of this task is to show students how working titles are flexible and developmental. It also gives them training in developing titles that are more specific and more academic in style.

4.2   Copy the titles and get students to compare their ideas about how the titles could be made more specific before showing them the sample answers on page 48. Explain that these are all authentic examples of titles used by pre-sessional students. See page 52 for a photocopiable handout.

Possible answers:

a)

Economics affects everything we do

↓

Economic factors affect our daily life in areas such as health care and education

↓

Economic factors, such as the cost of health care and education, have a hidden impact on daily life

↓

Economic forces have a significant hidden impact on social systems, such as health care

b)

The origin of genetic engineering

↓

The impact of genetic engineering on agricultural practice

↓

Genetic engineering in agricultural practice needs to be carefully controlled

c)

The effect of electronics on society

↓

The general impact of electronics on education

↓

The positive impact of electronic development on teaching methodology

It is worth discussing with the students how general or specific the final title is. The first example (a), on page 48, is obviously not general, because it deals with *specific* examples.

The second example (b) clearly comes under two main subheadings: *origin* and *importance*, and focus is established in this way.

The third example (c) would appear still to be very general. However, the writer may decide to interpret the title as a springboard for discussion, i.e., whether or not technology is important, how important it is, future developments in technology, etc.

4.3 This will probably be most effective if set initially as a homework task, so that students can go to the library or search the Internet independently. Obviously, foundation or undergraduate students may need more support with this task than postgraduates. Students should be encouraged to spend time planning and working out their ideas.

Task 5: Planning Project 2

Students often find it difficult to establish a focus for their project. The questions in the table act as guidelines to help them to do so. Encourage the students to complete the table as far as possible. This will probably need to be done as a homework task because students will need time to reflect.

In the following lesson, a brief class discussion should help students who have been unable to complete their planning for homework. This will also give students the opportunity to verbalize their ideas and thus clarify them.

You may wish to present the model below to students on an OHT for general discussion or for one-to-one tutorial work with students who are experiencing difficulty in formulating a plan (see page 53).

Planning Project 2: model notes

What is your topic?
The role of the family in 21st-century Turkey

Why have you chosen this topic?
- Academic subject = Sociology
- The role of the family is changing in Turkey (effects of globalization + transition from traditional model to 21st-century model)
- Impact on society is significant

Key questions (What do you want to find out about this topic?)
- Should the traditional role of the family in Turkey be retained?
- What are these 'traditional family values'?
- What are the positive and negative effects of retaining traditional family values/adopting modern family values?

What is your focus and/or working title?
In what way is the role of the traditional family having an impact on modern Turkish society?

Thesis statement
The changing role of the Turkish family is having a negative impact on social values. Change is inevitable but the rate of change is making the negative aspects difficult to control.

Specific title

The problems associated with the changing role of the Turkish family need to be urgently addressed for the 21st century

Unit summary

1   Answers:
   a) 2 or 6
   b) 1 (or 3)
   c) 5
   d) 4
   e) 3

2   Possible answers:
   a) Because a topic that is too general lacks focus. / Because you will be able to explore a topic in more depth.
   b) You can ask specific questions and narrow down the range. / You can rewrite the working title so that it is more specific.

3   Answers:
   a) establish a focus
   b) frequently
   c) being general to being specific

Web resources

The UVic writer's guide: planning, organizing and presenting essays
This section has a useful subsection entitled *Writing your essay: Getting started*. It gives tips on how to narrow down the topic and write a thesis statement. It also gives good and bad examples of a thesis.
http://web.uvic.ca/wguide/Pages/MasterToc.html

Using thesis statements
A short article that clarifies the role of thesis statements and dispels some myths about them. It also looks at characteristics of good and poor thesis statements.
http://www.utoronto.ca/writing/thesis.html

Additional online activities

Additional interactive activities to accompany this unit can be found online, at www.englishforacademicstudy.com.

Establishing a focus

Problems in the Chinese Economy
What is the chief economic problem facing China?
What effects is this problem having?
Who is causing the economic problems in China?
How serious are China's economic problems?

The economy of Taiwan
How stable is the Taiwanese economy?
What drives the Taiwanese economy?

Cybernetics
(Definition: *a branch of science which involves studying the way electronic machines and human brains work, and developing machines that do things or think rather like people. (Collins Cobuild 2001 English Dictionary).)*
What is cybernetics?
How important is the work carried out in this field?
Who are the stakeholders in the area of cybernetics?

The United Nations
What is the role of the United Nations?
How effective is the United Nations?
Which area of the United Nations' work has been the most successful?

Genetically modified (GM) food
How safe is GM food?
Why is food being genetically modified?
How is food genetically modified?

Deforestation in Nepal
What has caused deforestation in Nepal?
What have been the effects of deforestation?
How is the problem of deforestation being solved?

Future developments in human health
Which areas of human health will be dealt with in future?
What developments will occur?
How will developments in human health change?
Will developments in human health add to longevity?

Photocopiable

Establishing a working title

a)

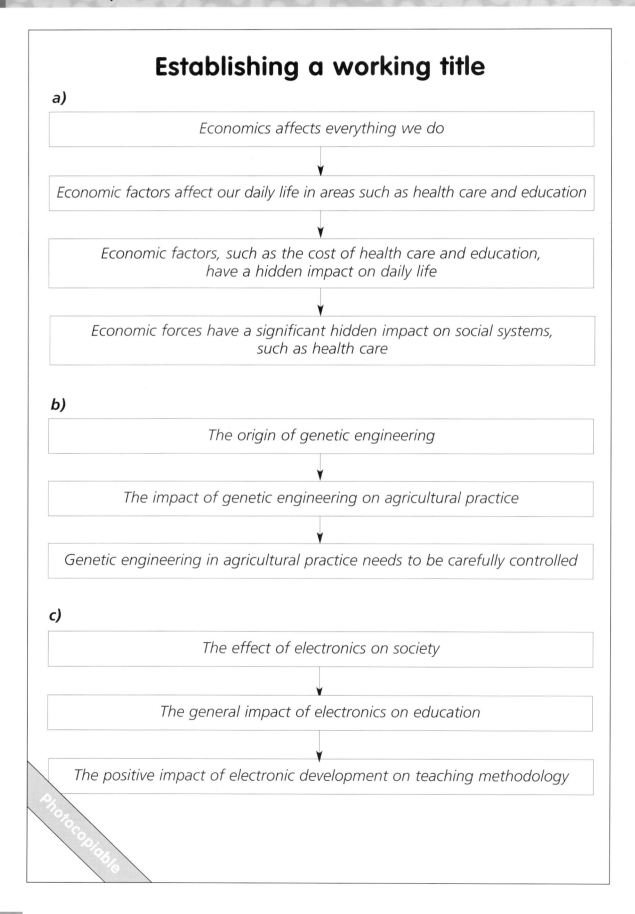

| Economics affects everything we do |

↓

| Economic factors affect our daily life in areas such as health care and education |

↓

| Economic factors, such as the cost of health care and education, have a hidden impact on daily life |

↓

| Economic forces have a significant hidden impact on social systems, such as health care |

b)

| The origin of genetic engineering |

↓

| The impact of genetic engineering on agricultural practice |

↓

| Genetic engineering in agricultural practice needs to be carefully controlled |

c)

| The effect of electronics on society |

↓

| The general impact of electronics on education |

↓

| The positive impact of electronic development on teaching methodology |

Photocopiable handout

Planning Project 2: model notes

What is your topic?

The role of the family in 21st-century Turkey

Why have you chosen this topic?

- Academic subject = Sociology
- The role of the family is changing in Turkey (effects of globalization + transition from traditional model to 21st-century model)
- Impact on society is significant

Key questions (What do you want to find out about this topic?)

- Should the traditional role of the family in Turkey be retained?
- What are these 'traditional family values'?
- What are the positive and negative effects of retaining traditional family values/adopting modern family values?

What is your focus and/or working title?

In what way is the role of the traditional family having an impact on modern Turkish society?

Thesis statement

The changing role of the Turkish family is having a negative impact on social values. Change is inevitable but the rate of change is making the negative aspects difficult to control.

Specific title

The problems associated with the changing role of the Turkish family need to be urgently addressed for the 21st century

Photocopiable

Introductions, conclusions and definitions

This unit will help students:
- analyze the features of introductions;
- analyze the features of conclusions;
- analyze the features of definitions;
- identify the language of each of these components in a typical academic text.

The purpose of this unit is to get students to look at certain aspects of their project. If your students are using *English for academic study: Writing*, they will be able to use the micro-skills they have been developing on the course as well as their experience of writing their project so far, including feedback. If students have written an introduction, ask them to bring a hard copy to class for Task 2. (Alternatively, they could bring a copy of the introduction to a previous project they have written.)

Writing introductions

Ask students what they already know about the features of introductions before you look at page 70. In small groups, get them to discuss the purpose of introductions. They may have covered this in *English for academic study: Writing*. After eliciting ideas (students should produce most of those on the Course Book list), look at the features on page 70 and explain Exercise 1.1.

Task 1: Features of introductions

1.1 Students should look at Introduction 1 and the accompanying table. This exercise should be discussed as a whole class. Emphasize that introductions may only have some of the features on page 70, depending on the writer's purpose.

1.2 Photocopy Introductions 2 to 4 (pages 71–72 of the Course Book) onto OHTs to make it easier to feed back on Task 1. See pages 66–67 of this book for photocopiable handouts, or www.englishforacademicstudy.com for PowerPoint files.

Answers:
Introduction 2

Feature	Example from text
introduction to topic (a)	*Since China began to develop economically and to open up to world trade in the early 1980s, many international companies have entered the Chinese market. In the beginning, these companies entered the market with confidence and kept their customary management system and market strategy approach.*
background information (b)	*Some of the European and American companies cooperated with Japanese companies, because they wanted to utilize the Japanese experience in the Asian market when marketing their products.* [This might also be included in the category above.]
justification (c)	*However, they soon found this approach was not suitable for the Chinese economic environment, and they had to find a way to adapt to the new situation.*
outline of structure (d)	*The issue of brand communication, including examining why this approach is necessary, and the steps involved in setting up promotion techniques to promote the prestige of a brand, will be discussed in this project.*
definition of key terms (e)	*They were interested in brand communication, which involves using a series of effective marketing strategies.*
thesis statement (f)	*This approach appears to work well in China.*
writer's purpose (g)	To show a way of solving the problem of marketing effectively in China (meaning inferred).

Introduction 3

Feature	Example from text
introduction to topic (a)	*Over the past decade, an uncertain economic climate and the rapid development of technology have led to an increasingly sophisticated business environment.*
background information (b)	[The example in the category above could also be considered background information.]
justification (c)	*Under these rapid changes, in order to gain competitive advantages, organizations are being increasingly reoriented or converged. ... Emphasis is on 'lean and mean' as an effective way for organizations to achieve the 'lean' purposes of downsizing.*
outline of structure (d)	*First, the purpose of downsizing will be addressed. Then, examples of the characteristics of an effective downsizing process will be examined. In the final part, three sets of data that evaluate the process of downsizing will be explored.*
definition of key terms (e)	*Downsizing (Steven et al., 1998) is a response to the external environment, as companies are attempting to reposition themselves so as to gain a competitive advantage in an uncertain marketplace.*
thesis statement (f)	*Downsizing is necessary for survival in many cases. If human resource managers lack an appropriate downsizing programme, they will be faced with negative feedback from employees. As a result, it will lead to the opposite effect to the 'lean' performance and efficient purposes of downsizing.*
writer's purpose (g)	*This project will examine how to present a positive vision of downsizing to employees.*

Introduction 4

Feature	Example from text
introduction to topic (a)	not included
background information (b)	not included
justification (c)	*But how does a company become global? Are there benefits to becoming a global company?* [These are rhetorical questions, which suggest that the writer is going to attempt to supply the answers. However, they could equally be considered an introduction to the topic – the questions raise the issues involved.]
outline of structure (d)	*This essay will first explain what a global company is, and then look at the difference between this and a non-global company. Secondly, the essay will explain global strategy and the benefits of global strategies. Finally, a case study of the globalizing development of Philips will be considered.*
definition of key terms (e)	*'Global' means worldwide.*
thesis statement (f)	not included
writer's purpose (g)	not included

As Introduction 4 does not have a thesis statement, you might ask students to suggest a suitable one.

Example:

Although there are many benefits to becoming a global company, there are also some drawbacks, and individual companies need to consider these before becoming globalized.

1.3 Answers:

Feature	Introduction 2	Introduction 3	Introduction 4
introduction to topic	✓	✓	
background information	✓		
justification	✓	✓	✓
outline of structure	✓	✓	✓
definition of key terms	✓	✓	✓
thesis statement	✓	✓	
writer's purpose	✓	✓	

Task 2: Analyzing your introduction

Answers will depend on students. Be prepared to discuss any extra features students may find in their introductions. If they are not in the list of features discussed above, it is probable that they should feature later in the essay, rather than in the introduction.

Task 3: The language of introductions

In this task, students are asked to look at Introductions 1–4 again and to identify typical expressions used in introductions. Constant reinforcement of the language development of the students is essential, and one way of doing this is to continuously raise awareness of language. Exposure to these expressions in context (rather than as isolated pieces of language) is important. Encourage discussion of the phrases that students identify and urge them to use this language in their own work.

You may wish to photocopy the summary of useful phrases at the end of this unit of the Teacher's Book, to use as a handout (see page 68).

Task 4: Identifying the thesis statement

4.1 Answers:

Coffee contains caffeine. `B`

Excessive amounts of caffeine can be damaging to health. `B`

Recent research, however, indicates that a limited amount of coffee can be beneficial. `T`

It stimulates the brain, aids concentration and may help to limit the effects of certain diseases such as Alzheimer's disease and Parkinson's disease. `E`

4.2
This is a good of example of where a thesis statement is not always obvious and is open for discussion. A brief discussion on this text should encourage students to engage in critical evaluation.

a) If anything, the thesis statement is contained in the fifth sentence: "the result has been that the rate of urban change has accelerated and new, distinctly different, urban forms have developed". This is because the following text will clearly attempt to demonstrate/prove this fact and show how the processes of urbanization are, in fact, "fundamentally different". This is, therefore, not a thesis statement of intent, but rather a hypothesis which the author sets out to prove. It may suggest an element of textual organization, i.e., a description/exemplification of urban changes followed by discussion to 'prove' the hypothesis. This is a fairly logical assumption of the likely organization.

b) Sentence 1: background information

Sentence 2: background information

Sentence 3: explanation

Sentence 4: explanation

Sentence 5: thesis statement

Sentence 6: example (this supports the thesis statement made in sentence 5)

4.3 You may wish to present the model answer below to students after they have completed Exercise 4.3, for comparison. It is worth pointing out that, very often, the thesis statement may be implied rather than explicitly stated. In the model answer, however, the thesis statement (underlined) is extended over two sentences. It is worth asking students what they think the implications might be, e.g., over-reliance on technology, less effort to learn and memorize (is this good or bad?), the need to develop greater critical awareness to compensate for the lost effort of memory retention, etc.

Model answer:

The onset of the 21st century has seen the full awakening of the age of requesting/accessing 'digital' information. Such knowledge seeking is manifested variously through powerful search engines or global positioning systems (satellite navigation); the verb 'google' has become synonymous with the idea of locating information. There is, however, a growing concern that anyone seeking information in this way is handing over responsibility for 'knowing geography' or, in fact, outsourcing the task to the internet for any access to general knowledge. The danger, it would appear, is that the concept of retaining knowledge in one's head is gradually becoming outmoded. This text will look at some of the implications of digital knowledge seeking, and will suggest possible short and longer-term outcomes.

Task 5: Features of conclusions

Writing conclusions
Note: You may like to work on this whole section (Tasks 5–7) at a different time if your students are not yet at the stage of writing their own conclusions.

As with the work on introductions, first elicit what the students know about the typical features of a conclusion, then direct them to the list in the Course Book.

5.1/5.2 After discussing the list of features from the Course Book with students, ask them to complete Exercise 5.1. With a weaker group, you might like to work through the features of Conclusion 1 as an example.

Photocopy Conclusions 1 to 4 (pages 76–78 of the Course Book) onto OHTs to make it easier to feed back on Tasks 5–7. The conclusions are reproduced as photocopiable handouts on pages 69–71 of this book, or go to www.englishforacademicstudy.com for PowerPoint files.

Answers:

Conclusion 1

Feature	Example from text
logical conclusion (a)	*… and thus MNCs will make a contribution to less developed countries through the development of transferable skills that can be applied to technological development, rather than using less developed countries purely for their own benefit.*
brief summary (b)	*However, certain conclusions can be drawn.* *Although investment into less developed countries by multinational corporations has many positive effects, there are also some problems. One of these is the problem of employee training. As mentioned in Section 3, with the present state of affairs, technology diffusion into developing countries via vocational training is not working effectively.* *Fortunately, as mentioned in Section 4, sophisticated companies have begun to realise their social responsibility, and recently have been trying to cooperate with governments and non-governmental organizations.* [There is overlap here between what might be considered comment and summary, as they are closely interwoven.]
comments on ideas (c)	*Whereas the aim of this essay was to evaluate the effect of technology transfer brought about by multinational corporations, (MNC), it has become a kind of summary of some researchers' theories …* *One possible reason is that MNCs have to protect their advantage of knowledge and investment-intensive technology in order not to lose their competitiveness in the market. The reason MNCs invest in less developed countries is to achieve the comparative advantage of low wages and cheap resources. Although vocational training is essential for multinational corporations to succeed in the markets of these countries, they do not directly aim to develop the level of technology in less developed countries. In other words, the progress of technology in less developed countries is the secondary product of multinational enterprises. The original idea that this technology would transfer beyond efficient employee training for a specific purpose seems to have been an idealistic theoretical concept. However, if this situation is not changed, the technological gap between developed countries and developing countries will increase, leading to a widening of the gap between rich developed countries and poor developing countries.* *Fortunately, as mentioned in Section 4, sophisticated companies have begun to realise their social responsibility, and recently have been trying to cooperate with governments and non-governmental organizations.*
predictions (d)	*It is to be hoped that this trend will continue …*
further research (e)	not included
limitations (f)	not included
reference to thesis statement (g)	*whereas the aim of this essay was to evaluate the effect of technology transfer brought about by multinational corporations …* *It is to be hoped that this trend will continue …*

Conclusion 2

Feature	Example from text
logical conclusion (a)	*Only well-planned appropriate technology that takes these factors into consideration will work in solving the serious energy problems in remote areas.*
brief summary (b)	*Industrialized countries have received a considerable number of benefits from energy, especially electricity, and the demand for energy has been increasing. However, as discussed above, there are still many people who do not have access to electric light, as a conventional energy supply system is not suitable in remote areas.*
comments on ideas (c)	*Nevertheless, even if renewable energy technologies are applied, it is not easy to establish the technology in poor societies. When this technology is applied, the concept of appropriate technology is extremely important. The designer needs to grasp the economic, technical, social and cultural background of the area. He/she also needs to think of the characteristics of each technology, as well as climatic conditions.*
predictions (d)	*In order to solve the energy crisis in remote areas, renewable energy technology has great potential.*
further research (e)	not included
limitations (f)	*Although only two kinds of technologies have been examined in this work, other renewable energy technologies are advantageous, and these technologies have also been accepted in some areas as a main energy supply system.*
reference to thesis statement (g)	*He/she also needs to think of the characteristics of each technology, as well as climatic conditions. Only well-planned appropriate technology that takes these factors into consideration will work in solving the serious energy problems in remote areas.*

Conclusion 3

Feature	Example from text
logical conclusion (a)	not included
brief summary (b)	*This essay has discussed the features of language aptitude. It has emerged that language aptitude is often applied to the classroom situation, but not in real-life situations. As second language acquisition is such a complicated process, it is necessary to explore the influence of age, motivation, attitude, personality and the mother tongue, in order to understand the process more fully.*
comments on ideas (c)	not included
predictions (d)	not included
further research (e)	*It would be interesting to examine how these factors can influence language learning, and compensate for the natural aptitude that learners possess to a greater or lesser extent, as this project has shown.* [This might also be construed as a 'limitation' of the present study.]
limitations (f)	not included
reference to thesis statement (g)	*... and compensate for the natural aptitude that learners possess to a greater or lesser extent*

Conclusion 4

Feature	Example from text
logical conclusion (a)	*Eventually, encouraged by nationwide consensus, the new government dared to challenge the tough task of restructuring the banking system.*
brief summary (b)	*In the spate of bank crises in Asia, Korea's banking system also suffered the hardest time in its history. Seventeen commercial banks were closed and more than 40,000 bank employees were expelled from their companies. It cost 137.1 trillion won (equivalent to 110 billion US dollars) to restore the banking system.*
comments on ideas (c)	*The crisis was inevitable because it was an eruption of deep-rooted problems, such as policy mistakes and poor bank management. However, Korea's banks successfully weathered the crisis. As of June 2002, Korea's banks recorded an historically high net profit, and their capital structures are the soundest in the world. There are a number of factors which contributed to this success. Of these success factors, the following seem to be key. First, the Korean government followed many valuable lessons suggested by empirical studies. For example, it set up prompt and massive action plans, including a huge amount of public funds. It also maintained its strict stances at all times. It introduced a considerable number of standard global regulations and incentive systems to enhance the competition. Secondly, change in the political power of the time played a key role in implementing strict policies for restructuring. As the new government was relatively free from responsibility for the crisis and political interests, they could undertake firm action. Thirdly, nationwide consensus for changes strongly supported government reforms. The Korean people knew that change was needed in order to survive.*
predictions (d)	*Future prospects are good.*
further research (e)	not included
limitations (f)	not included
reference to thesis statement (g)	*There are a number of factors which contributed to this success …*

5.3   Answers:

Feature	Conclusion 1	Conclusion 2	Conclusion 3	Conclusion 4
logical conclusion	✓	✓		✓
brief summary	✓	✓	✓	✓
comments on ideas	✓	✓		✓
predictions	✓	✓		✓
further research			✓	
limitations		✓		
reference to thesis statement	✓	✓	✓	✓

Task 6: Analyzing your conclusion

Leave this task until students have completed the conclusions to their projects. Be prepared to discuss any extra features students might find in their conclusions. If they are not in the list of features discussed above, it is possible that they should be included in an earlier section of the essay.

Task 7: The language of conclusions

In this task, students are asked to look at Conclusions 1–4 again, and identify typical expressions used in conclusions. Encourage discussion of the phrases that students identify, and urge them to use this language in their own work, as before.

You may wish to photocopy the summary of useful phrases at the end of this unit of the Teacher's Book, to use as a handout (see page 72).

Task 8: Features of definitions

It is important to emphasize that definitions have different features according to their purpose. As with introductions and conclusions, it is a good idea to elicit what students already know about the features of definitions, based on their experience of writing essays so far.

Make sure that the students are aware that 'expansion' could refer to exemplification or explanation.

8.2 Answers:

Feature	Definition 1	Definition 2	Definition 3	Definition 4
formal definition	✓	✓	✓	✓
expansion	✓	✓	✓	✓
comment	✓	✓	✓	
references	✓	✓	✓	✓

8.3 Answers:

Definition 1

Feature	Example from text
formal definition	*A factor which makes a difference to the individual is often referred to as language aptitude. Though difficult to define in concrete terms, it is understood to be not necessarily the ability to learn the language in the classroom, but rather to be able to apply this knowledge in a real-life situation (Cook, 1991).*
expansion	*While some people argue that this ability is not fixed, Carroll (1981) believes that aptitude is an innate or stable factor, which cannot be changed through training and is constant throughout one's life. He also insists that it is not related to past learning experience.*
comment	*This implies that language aptitude is not something that is accumulated as we age, but something we are born with. This may sound demotivating for those who are not equipped with language aptitude and struggle to acquire a basic communicative ability in the language.* *However, as Ellis (1994) suggests, aptitude is only a facilitator which encourages learning, especially accelerating the rate of learning, but not determining learning.*
references	three references

Definition 2

Feature	Example from text
formal definition	It refers to 'the idea that the world is developing a single economy and culture as a result of improved technology and communications and the influence of very large multinational companies ' (Macmillan English dictionary for advanced learners, 2000, p. 603).
expansion	The term can also refer to the movement of people (labour) and knowledge (technology) across international borders. Globalization can help countries get rid of the barriers to the inflow of technology, capital, human resources and products.
comment	Generally, globalization makes the above more available, especially the accessibility of products. It can also speed up the development of foreign trade.
references	one reference

Definition 3

Feature	Example from text
formal definition	A global company can be defined as a corporation consisting of a group of people who run a business in different countries as one body (Uniglobe, 2002).
expansion	There are three main differences between a global company and a non-global company. First of all, a global company should introduce its same-brand products worldwide at the same time. Secondly, a global company must inform its subsidiaries around the world of major management decisions. Thirdly, each subsidiary of the global company based in a different country must compete at a national level by taking local preferences into consideration.
comment	A global company is different from a non-global company.
references	one reference

Definition 4

Feature	Example from text
formal definition	The term 'global' (or 'transnational') implies the centralization of management decision-making to overseas subsidiaries and highly efficient coordination of activities across national boundaries in pursuit of global competitiveness (Yip, 1992; Bartlett and Ghoshol, 1989).
expansion	A multinational business refers to a company with branches in several countries with little coordination of activities, and decentralization of management decision-making (Bartlett & Ghoshol, 1989).
comment	not included
references	two references

Highlight the useful phrases in Definitions 1–4, as below, for example.

Definition 1

… is often referred to as …
… it is understood to be …
While some people argue …
Caroll (1981) believes that aptitude is …
This implies that …
… as Ellis (1994) suggests, aptitude is …

Definition 2
The term can also refer to …

Definition 3
A global company can be defined as …
There are three main differences between a global company and a non-global company.

Definition 4
The term 'global' (or 'transnational') implies …

8.4   Answers:

In this case, the most useful definition would appear to be Definition 1: Language aptitude, since:
- it compares several sources;
- it comments on the sources by looking at the implications.

This will probably provoke discussion. Students should be encouraged to fully justify their choices.

Some useful ideas to note
- A simple definition with no comment or explanation by the writer is not particularly useful.
- Exemplification (expanding with examples) is a useful way of clarifying the meaning of the term being defined.
- References give academic 'weight' to a definition.
- A comment by the writer shows s/he has really thought about the definition.
- A definition that draws on several sources, both commenting on them and using them as the basis of the term to be used in the essay, shows evidence of critical thinking.

8.5   Remind students that their definition should be written for the 'educated reader', e.g., someone who would read *New Scientist* or a similar serious and informative publication intended for general readers. The reader should not need to have specialist knowledge of the topic in order to understand the definition. This task may be set for homework and looked at in the next class.

Unit summary

1   Answers:
a) I
b) C
c) I
d) C
e) C
f) I
g) I
h) C
i) I
j) I
k) C

3   Answers:
When you are writing about a topic you must clarify your <u>terms</u> (explain clearly what you mean by any key words you use) so that the writer and the reader have the same <u>interpretation</u>. If you are new to the subject, you will need to clarify the most basic terms so that you understand them properly. As you gain <u>knowledge</u> of the subject, and if you are writing for experts, the meaning of certain key terms can be assumed as part of <u>shared knowledge</u>. You can use formal definitions from a <u>dictionary</u> or an expert in the field, expand a definition with explanations or <u>examples</u>, or make a <u>comment</u> about the definition.

Web resources

University of Essex: my skills: introduction and conclusion writing
These pages explain the features of introductions and conclusions in academic writing and give help and tips on how to write them. Each section includes a task to review and reinforce the information in the section.
http://www.essex.ac.uk/myskills/skills/writing/introConclWriting.asp

Language and learning online: defining your topic
A summary of how to use definitions (formal/informal and expanded definitions), together with examples and practice in identifying techniques used in writing definitions.
http://www.monash.edu.au/lls/llonline/writing/general/thesis-edit/2.2.xml

Additional online activities

Additional interactive activities to accompany this unit can be found online, at www.englishforacademicstudy.com.

Introduction 1

The application of renewable energy technology in remote areas

Our life is heavily dependent on the supply of energy. After World War II, especially, developed countries received the great benefits of electricity. However, today more than 30% of the global population still live in off-grid areas, without electricity. This is mostly in developing countries or remote parts of developed countries, such as mountainous areas or isolated islands. Economically, it would be very challenging to produce electricity for these areas. As developing countries grow economically, the demand for energy will increase rapidly, thus adding to the pollution problems caused by fossil fuels. Renewable energy technology is the solution to these problems. This essay will first demonstrate the need for electricity in remote areas, and then the extent to which renewable energy technology can meet this need in remote areas will be examined by looking at some examples.

Introduction 2

Brand communication in China

Since China began to develop economically and to open up to world trade in the early 1980s, many international companies have entered the Chinese market. In the beginning, these companies entered the market with confidence and kept their customary management system and market strategy approach. However, they soon found this approach was not suitable for the Chinese economic environment, and they had to find a way to adapt to the new situation. Some of the European and American companies cooperated with Japanese companies, because they wanted to utilize the Japanese experience in the Asian market when marketing their products. They were interested in brand communication, which involves using a series of effective marketing strategies. This approach appears to work well in China. The issue of brand communication, including examining why this approach is necessary, and the steps involved in setting up promotion techniques to promote the prestige of a brand, will be discussed in this project.

Photocopiable

Photocopiable handout

Introduction 3

Downsizing as a necessity for survival

Over the past decade, an uncertain economic climate and the rapid development of technology have led to an increasingly sophisticated business environment. Under these rapid changes, in order to gain competitive advantages, organizations are being increasingly reoriented or converged. Downsizing (Steven et al. 1998) is a response to the external environment, as companies are attempting to reposition themselves so as to gain a competitive advantage in an uncertain marketplace. Emphasis is on 'lean and mean' as an effective way for organisations to achieve the 'lean' purposes of downsizing. Downsizing is necessary for survival in many cases. If human resource managers lack an appropriate downsizing programme, they will be faced with negative feedback from employees. This will lead to the opposite effect to the 'lean' performance and efficient purposes of downsizing. This project will examine how to present a positive vision of downsizing to employees. First, the purpose of downsizing will be addressed. Then, examples of the characteristics of an effective downsizing process will be examined. In the final part, three sets of data that evaluate the process of downsizing will be explored.

Introduction 4

The development of a global company

'Global' means worldwide. But how does a company become global? Are there benefits to becoming a global company? This essay will first explain what a global company is, and then look at the difference between this and a non-global company. Secondly, the essay will explain global strategy and the benefits of these strategies. Finally, a case study of the globalizing development of Philips will be considered.

The language of introductions

Introduction to topic

But how does a company become global?
Are there benefits to becoming a global company?
(Introduction 4)

Background information

After World War II … However, today … This is mostly …
(Introduction 1)
Over the past decade … have led to … (Introduction 3)

Outline of structure

This essay will first demonstrate … and then the extent to which … will be examined by looking at some examples.
(Introduction 1)
The issue of … including examining why … will be discussed in this project. (Introduction 2)
First … will be addressed. Then … will be examined. In the final part, … will be explored. (Introduction 3)
This essay will first explain … Finally, a case study … will be considered. (Introduction 4)

Definition of key terms

'Global' means worldwide. (Introduction 4)

Writer's purpose

This project will examine how … (Introduction 3)

Conclusion 1

The impact of technology transfer by multinational corporations

Whereas the aim of this essay was to evaluate the effect of technology transfer brought about by multinational corporations (MNCs), it has become a kind of summary of some researchers' theories. However, certain conclusions can be drawn.

Although investment into less developed countries by multinational corporations has many positive effects, there are also some problems. One of these is the problem of employee training. As mentioned in Section 3, with the present state of affairs, technology diffusion into developing countries via vocational training is not working effectively. One possible reason is that MNCs have to protect their advantage of knowledge and investment-intensive technology in order not to lose their competitiveness in the market. The reason MNCs invest in less developed countries is to achieve the comparative advantage of low wages and cheap resources. Although vocational training is essential for multinational corporations to succeed in the markets of these countries, they do not directly aim to develop the level of technology in less developed countries. In other words, the progress of technology in less developed countries is the secondary product of multinational enterprises. The original idea that this technology would transfer beyond efficient employee training for a specific purpose seems to have been an idealistic theoretical concept. However, if this situation is not changed, the technological gap between developed countries and developing countries will increase, leading to a widening of the gap between rich developed countries and poor developing countries.

Fortunately, as mentioned in Section 4, sophisticated companies have begun to realize their social responsibility, and recently have been trying to cooperate with governments and non-governmental organizations. It is to be hoped that this trend will continue, and thus MNCs will make a contribution to less developed countries through the development of transferable skills that can be applied to technological development, rather than using less developed countries purely for their own benefit.

Conclusion 2

The application of renewable energy technology in remote areas

Industrialized countries have received a considerable number of benefits from energy, especially electricity, and the demand for energy has been increasing. However, as discussed above, there are still many people who do not have access to electric light, as a conventional energy supply system is not suitable in remote areas. In order to solve the energy crisis in remote areas, renewable energy technology has great potential. Although only two kinds of technologies have been examined in this work, other renewable energy technologies are advantageous, and these technologies have also been accepted in some areas as a main energy supply system. Nevertheless, even if renewable energy technologies are applied, it is not easy to establish the technology in poor societies. When this technology is applied, the concept of appropriate technology is extremely important. The designer needs to grasp the economic, technical, social and cultural background of the area. He/she also needs to think of the characteristics of each technology, as well as climatic conditions. Only well-planned appropriate technology that takes these factors into consideration will work in solving the serious energy problems in remote areas.

Conclusion 3

Language aptitude as a factor in second language learning

This essay has discussed the features of language aptitude. It has emerged that language aptitude is often applied to the classroom situation, but not in real-life situations. As second language acquisition is such a complicated process, it is necessary to explore the influence of age, motivation, attitude, personality and the mother tongue, in order to understand the process more fully. It would be interesting to examine how these factors can influence language learning, and compensate for the natural aptitude that learners possess to a greater or lesser extent, as this project has shown.

Conclusion 4

Why was the restructuring of the Korean banking system successful?

In the spate of bank crises in Asia, Korea's banking system also suffered the hardest time in its history. Seventeen commercial banks were closed and more than 40,000 bank employees were expelled from their companies. It cost 137.1 trillion won (equivalent to 110 billion US dollars) to restore the banking system. The crisis was inevitable because it was an eruption of deep-rooted problems, such as policy mistakes and poor bank management. However, Korea's banks successfully weathered the crisis. As of June 2002, Korea's banks recorded an historically high net profit, and their capital structures are the soundest in the world. Future prospects are good.

There are a number of factors which contributed to this success. Of these success factors, the following seem to be key. First, the Korean government followed many valuable lessons suggested by empirical studies. For example, it set up prompt and massive action plans, including a huge amount of public funds. It introduced a considerable number of standard global regulations and incentive systems in order to be competitive. Secondly, change in the political power of the time played a key role in implementing strict policies for restructuring. As the new government was relatively free from responsibility for the crisis and political interests, they could undertake firm action. Thirdly, nationwide consensus for changes strongly supported government reforms. The Korean people knew that change was needed in order to survive. Eventually, encouraged by nationwide consensus, the new government dared to challenge the tough task of restructuring the banking system.

The language of conclusions

Logical conclusion

... and thus ... (Conclusion 1)
Eventually ... (Conclusion 4)

Brief summary

As mentioned in Section 3 ... (Conclusion 1)
However, as discussed above ... (Conclusion 2)
This essay has discussed ... (Conclusion 3)
It has emerged that ... (Conclusion 3)
First ... Secondly ... Thirdly ... (Conclusion 4)

Comments on ideas

Whereas the aim of this essay was to evaluate ... it has become a summary of the theories of some researchers (Conclusion 1)
There are a number of factors which contributed to ... (Conclusion 4)

Predictions

It is to be hoped that ... will ... (Conclusion 1)
Only ... which take these factors into consideration will work ... (Conclusion 2)
Future prospects are ... (Conclusion 4)

Further research

It would be interesting to examine ... (Conclusion 3)

Limitations

Although only ... have been examined in this work ... (Conclusion 2)

7 Incorporating data and illustrations

This unit will help students:
● learn how data is incorporated into academic texts;
● learn how to analyze data;
● practise using the language of data commentary.

Before students begin Task 1, try to elicit the ideas outlined below, either with a brainstorming session in small groups or as a whole-class activity, i.e., What is data? What is the purpose of data? What is the purpose of using pictures or diagrams? Why and when should students use data or illustrations in their projects? Students can then write down the results of the brainstorming in Task 1.

What is data?

Tables

Tables usually consist of listed information, e.g., a list of African cities with their comparative populations over three decades, for example, 1980, 1990 and 2000, set out in three columns. You could copy the following table on to the board as an example:

Table 1.1: Urban population growth in major African urban areas

City	1980	1990	2000
Cape Town	1.5m	2.3m	2.9m
Lusaka	1.0m	1.6m	2.8m

You may wish to point out that the caption that goes with tabulated data should go above the table. However, captions that accompany figures should go below the figure. Get students to remember the word *tabletop*, as this may help them remember this rule about the position of captions.

Figures

Figures can be charts, graphs, maps, photographs, diagrams, etc.

Why is data sometimes included in academic texts?

Emphasize that data can serve a number of purposes. Elicit these and list them on the board, if appropriate. Some examples of why data is included in academic texts might be:
● to summarize information concisely;
● to clarify the content of the text;
● to provide a source of evidence to support claims made in the text;
● to show the results of experiments or other forms of research, such as the results of questionnaires that a researcher has distributed.

It is important to reiterate the following statement from the Course Book: *Only include data or illustrations if they have a purpose.* There is a tendency for students to include data or illustrations in their projects haphazardly, either as a result of anxiety or because they have seen other students include data in their work. It is an aspect of a student's work that could be discussed during a one-to-one tutorial. (The tutor may ask *Explain why you have included this table here.*)

It is also important for students to consider the positioning of any data that they include in their work.

The data must be as close to the reference in the text as possible. It is sometimes more appropriate to include certain data in an appendix. This must be referenced in the text.

Examples of why data or illustrations might be included in an appendix rather than in the main body of text can be discussed. For example:
- the size (e.g., a map of the world);
- the number (too many tables and graphs make it difficult for the reader to follow the text);
- the requirements of a particular university department or subject area.

Task 1: The purpose of data

Remind students to refer back to these pages if they decide to include data and/or illustrations in their own projects.

1.1 Possible answers:

a) Data is information in the form of facts or statistics that can be analyzed.
b) Data is included to:
- clarify an idea or argument (make it more understandable);
- give weight to an argument or hypothesis;
- summarize information in a concise and accessible way.

c) 1 Figure 1.21 shows an example.
2 Figure 1.22 summarizes facts about the gross output of tourism during the specified period.
3 The main conclusion from Figure 1.22 is that output grew steadily during this period.
4 Table 1.5 summarizes in simple terms the number of tourist arrivals worldwide and the percentage rate of growth.
5 The main conclusions from Table 1.5 are that tourist arrivals grew during this period; the two exceptions coincided with periods of conflict – the Falklands War and the 'First' Gulf War.

1.2 Possible answers:
a) The language style is like headlines, i.e., no articles or verbs; concise language using key words.
b) The position of the caption depends on the type of illustration. For tables, the caption goes above (*tabletop*); for figures, the caption goes below.

Task 2: The language used for incorporating data

2.1 Students should highlight examples of language, working on their own and then comparing in pairs, or working in pairs throughout.

Answers:
... (see figure 1.21)
Figure 1.22 below shows ...
... is illustrated in Table 1.5
Table 1.5 indicates ...
Figure 1.23 shows ...

2.2 Answers:
1 is a table; 2, 3 and 4 are figures.

2.3/2.4 **Answers:**
a) *Household take-up of digital television: by type of service* matches Data 3.
b) *Selected media activities that would be missed the most: by age, 2008* matches Data 4.

2.5 **Possible answers:**
Data 1: Readership of national daily newspapers
Data 2: Radio listening: by age, 2007

2.6 **Possible answers:**
See references to each piece of data in the text below (in bold). It is important to explain that this is a sample answer. You could copy this sample answer and display and/or hand it out for general discussion. See page 78 for a photocopiable handout.

In 2008, the 'digital switchover' began. Data from Ofcom **(Figure 2)** shows that nearly 87 per cent of homes in the UK had a digital television service at the end of the first quarter in 2008, a rise of 71 percentage points since 2000. A digital television set can also transmit digital radio stations. According to Radio Joint Audience Research Limited **(Figure 1)**, the average time spent listening to the radio by people in the UK in the first quarter of 2007 was 19 hours and 24 minutes per week; average listening time increases with age. Between 2001/02 and 2006/07, radio listening fell among most age groups. **With reference to Table 1, it is clear that** the proportion of people reading a daily newspaper has also been declining for a number of years. The National Readership Survey shows that, on an average day, less than 44 per cent of people aged 15 and over in Great Britain read a national daily newspaper in the 12 months to June 2008, compared with 72 per cent in the 12 months to June 1978. In 2007, Ofcom asked which media activity respondents would miss the most if they were all taken away **(Figure 3)**. Watching television would be the most-missed activity for all age groups except those aged 16 to 19, who would miss the mobile phone the most.

Task 3: Data commentary

3.2 Get students to study and talk about Table 1: Asian students at the Oceanic School in small groups. Ask them how they would organize their data commentary, e.g., from general to specific. Students should then attempt a description of the data – working individually or in pairs. They should only write about the most significant trends displayed by the data and should use the sort of language they have been introduced to in the previous two tasks. Refer the students to the data commentary flow chart. Point out that they will have a further opportunity to practise data commentary in Task 5.

The data commentary flow chart suggests five steps to successfully referencing data. One feature of this step-by-step approach is that it produces commentary organized from the general to the specific. The step-by-step approach also offers opportunities for comparison of features of the data and for consideration of the implications or reasons for certain trends.

The model description below follows the steps in the flow chart. Copy the model onto an OHT or distribute it as a handout for discussion (see page 79).

Model data commentary:
Table 1 shows the country of origin of Asian students studying at the Oceanic School. There has been a sharp increase in the number of students from Asia; the number has almost trebled since 1999. This is particularly evident in the past two years, with the huge increase in the number of Chinese students. The number of students from Japan has fallen steadily. This increase in the number of Chinese students is the result of a number of factors, perhaps including the more open policy of the Chinese government, which has made the process of obtaining a visa to study abroad less complex than in the past.

Task 4: The language of data commentary

Possible answers:

Column A: Nouns	Column B: Verb forms	Column C: Accompanying adjective/adverb
rise	rise/rose/has risen	• a steady rise • rose steadily
increase	increase/increased/has increased	• rapid increase • increased rapidly
fall	fall/fell/has fallen	• a dramatic fall • fell dramatically
drop	drop/dropped/has dropped	• a noticeable drop • dropped noticeably
decrease	decrease/decreased/has decreased	• a significant decrease • decreased significantly
stability	stabilize/stabilized/has stabilized	• gradual stability • stabilized gradually
fluctuation	fluctuate/fluctuated/has fluctuated	• an unexpected fluctuation • fluctuated unexpectedly

4.3 **Possible answers:**

slight/slightly	a slight increase
frequent/frequently	a frequent fluctuation
occasional/occasionally	an occasional rise
alarming/alarmingly	dropped alarmingly

Task 5: Practice data commentary

Get students to work on this individually before small-group or whole-group discussion. Explain that the example below is a model answer and that other versions will be just as acceptable. See page 80 for a photocopiable handout.

Model data commentary:

Employment in the manufacturing and service industries
Figure 1 displays data over a 30-year period (1978–2008), comparing the number of people employed in the manufacturing and service industries and also showing the difference in male and female employment. During this period, there were significantly more people employed in the service sector, and the numbers increased steadily. However, the numbers in manufacturing declined. It is noteworthy that there were more female employees in the service industries than males and that the gap seems to have expanded slightly. Conversely, there were a greater number of males employed in manufacturing throughout the period. Numerically, the gender gap, if anything, increased between the two sectors. This may have reflected a global trend, or at least have been in line with the general trend in the developed world.

It is worth using this model to get students to identify certain features of a data commentary, e.g., the introduction to the subject of the data (sentence 1); a general comment on the main trend (sentence 2); a comment on some of the significant features (sentence 3). There is implicit comparison running through the commentary and implications are suggested in sentence 4.

Point out that only a limited amount of significant data is commented on. The reader can draw other conclusions for her/himself by viewing the data. Explain that data is often displayed simply to emphasize a particular point; here, for example, the writer might have been suggesting concern about employment or industrial policy in the UK.

Unit summary

1   Answer:
Statement d is not true.

3   Possible answers:
   a) rise / increase
   b) fall / decrease / drop
   c) fluctuate / stabilize
   d) rise / increase / fall / decrease / drop
   e) steady / dramatic / rapid / slow / significant / unexpected / noticeable
   f) steadily / dramatically / rapidly / slowly / significantly / unexpectedly / noticeably

Web resources

CILL: describing trends
Hong Kong Polytechnic University's Centre for Independent Language Learning introduces the vocabulary and grammar needed to describe trends. It is followed by a gap-fill exercise to test your ability to use the language.
http://elc.polyu.edu.hk/CILL/exercises/trends.htm

University of Manchester: the academic phrasebank
These pages list useful phrases for each of the stages of data commentary, including useful phrases for contrasting, discussing significant features and commenting on results.
http://www.phrasebank.manchester.ac.uk/

Additional online activities

Additional interactive activities to accompany this unit can be found online, at www.englishforacademicstudy.com.

The language used for incorporating data

In 2008, the 'digital switchover' began. Data from Ofcom **(Figure 2)** shows that nearly 87 per cent of homes in the UK had a digital television service at the end of the first quarter in 2008, a rise of 71 percentage points since 2000. A digital television set can also transmit digital radio stations. According to Radio Joint Audience Research Limited **(Figure 1)**, the average time spent listening to the radio by people in the UK in the first quarter of 2007 was 19 hours and 24 minutes per week; average listening time increases with age. Between 2001/02 and 2006/07, radio listening fell among most age groups. **With reference to Table 1, it is clear that** the proportion of people reading a daily newspaper had also been declining for a number of years. The National Readership Survey shows that, on an average day, less than 44 per cent of people aged 15 and over in Great Britain read a national daily newspaper in the 12 months to June 2008, compared with 72 per cent in the 12 months to June 1978. In 2007, Ofcom asked which media activity respondents would miss the most if they were all taken away **(Figure 3)**. Watching television would be the most-missed activity for all age groups except those aged 16 to 19, who would miss the mobile phone the most.

Adapted from: Self, A. (Ed.). (2008). *Social trends 38 – 2008 edition* and Hughes, M. (Ed.). (2009). *Social trends 39 – 2009 edition*. Retrieved April 21, 2009, from National Statistics Online: http://www.statistics.gov.uk

Model data commentary

Asian students at the Oceanic School

Table 1 shows the country of origin of Asian students studying at the Oceanic School. There was a sharp increase in the number of students from Asia between 1999 and 2003; the number almost trebled. This was particularly evident from 2002, with the huge increase in the number of Chinese students. The number of students from Japan fell steadily. This increase in the number of Chinese students was the result of a number of factors, perhaps including the more open policy of the Chinese government, which made the process of obtaining a visa to study abroad less complex than before.

Model data commentary

Employment in the manufacturing and service industries

Figure 1 displays data over a 30-year period (1978–2008), comparing the number of people employed in the manufacturing and service industries and also showing the difference in male and female employment. During this period, there were significantly more people employed in the service sector, and the numbers increased steadily. However, the numbers in manufacturing declined. It is noteworthy that there were more female employees in the service industries than males and that the gap seems to have expanded slightly. Conversely, there were a greater number of males employed in manufacturing throughout the period. Numerically, the gender gap, if anything, increased between the two sectors. This may have reflected a global trend, or at least have been in line with the general trend in the developed world.

8 Preparing for conference presentations and editing your work

This unit will help students:
- analyze, evaluate and practise writing abstracts;
- prepare for an oral presentation using note cards and OHTs or PowerPoint;
- learn how to prepare a poster presentation;
- edit the final draft of their project.

In this unit, students will write two abstracts: one for their written project and one for a conference presentation. The abstract for the written project should be between 100 and 150 words in length.

Writing abstracts

Students have already been introduced to abstracts in Unit 4. Get them to read through the introduction to Unit 8 and then look back at Unit 4, as necessary.

Task 1: Features of abstracts

1.1 This exercise gives students further practice in identifying the features of an abstract and acts as useful revision.

Answers:

Feature	Abstract 1	Abstract 2
a	✓	✓
b	✓	✓
c	✓	✓
d	✓	✓
e		✓
f	✓	✓
g		
h		✓
i	✓	✓
j	✓	✓

1.2/1.3 Writing an abstract from memory is a useful way to focus on key points. Stress that students should write on the lines provided (this limits the length of their abstract). After they have written their abstract, students can exchange and peer-evaluate them, identifying the typical features of abstracts they discussed in Exercise 1.1.

Task 2: Conference abstracts

A good conference abstract typically has the following characteristics:
- precision of expression;
- concise reference to key points;
- a summary of the whole project, including the main conclusion.

It is essential to remember that an abstract helps the reader decide whether to attend a presentation at all. The text of the abstract must therefore be accessible.

2.1 **Answers:**
Abstract A: *Situation analysis in marketing*
Abstract B: *Interpretation and analysis of financial statements for non-accountants*
Abstract C: *Communication management in Transmission Control Protocol (TCP)*
Abstract D: *Mixed-use developments in the Kingdom of Saudi Arabia*
Abstract E: *Foreign investment in China*
Abstract F: *Banking systems and management: challenges facing Taiwanese banks*

2.2 Explain that the number of words a conference speaker can use for an abstract is restricted. This is usually because the conference programme has only very limited space for each speaker to outline the key points of their paper.

Set a limit of 60 words. Encourage students to begin with key words from their project. They should then draft and redraft their abstract as necessary, so that they say all they have to say concisely and effectively within the word limit.

Task 3: Preparing an oral presentation

The amount of guidance that students receive on giving presentations can vary widely from department to department of a university. There is also variation in the methods and criteria used for assessing presentations. Students on the pre-sessional course at the University of Reading are given opportunities to develop presentation skills in a dedicated 'Spoken Language class'. For this reason, the work on oral presentation skills in this book is limited. Students are simply reminded about the use of note cards, OHTs and posters in the rest of this unit.

It might be most appropriate for students to give an oral presentation about an aspect of their project, rather than trying to describe the whole project.

One way of doing this is to organize a mini-conference towards the end of the course, where each student gives a presentation in front of her/his peers and teachers. For example, 10–12 minutes could be allowed for each presentation, with 3 minutes for questions. Depending on numbers and time, this can be organized in parallel sessions over a single day, or sequentially over several days.

An alternative would be for individuals to present stages of their project to smaller groups. This can be an effective way for students to keep to deadlines and for them to focus on the content and organization of their project as they progress through the various stages of drafting.

There might be sufficient time for both the end-of-course conference and the ongoing approach to be implemented. See page 89 of this book for a presentation assessment form.

3.1/3.2 Give students time to think about and discuss the note card.

Mention the following points.
- Note form is used.
- There is plenty of space between each note, for ease of reference.
- Different notation is used to help the reader distinguish between types of information, i.e., a main heading followed by main points a, b and c.

Explain that note cards can be very effective resources. They can be used when giving presentations, but also for noting bibliographical details in the library, for examination revision notes, etc.

3.3 Get students to analyze the project titles and prepare a set of note cards on just one of them.

Possible answers:
See the examples on page 85. You could photocopy these for comparison and general discussion.

Students must understand that the most successful PowerPoint slides or OHTs are simple and clear. They have to be 'reader-friendly'. There should be plenty of space between each line of text.

3.4 **Answers:**
  a) The layouts of the note card and the OHT/slide are quite similar (both have a main heading and lettered sub-points).
  b) The most obvious difference between the note card and the OHT/slide is the incorporation of the Cohen definition on the slide (note the reference) and the more professional appearance of the type on the slide.

Ask students what else can be displayed successfully on an OHT/slide. Some examples are: data (graphs, tables, etc.), maps, diagrams and flow charts.

Editing your written work
Students often submit a final draft of their project without checking it carefully. This is usually due to poor time management skills and the pressure of completing work before the end of the course. Emphasize that even native speakers allow time for editing and checking their work carefully.

Refer students to the checklist on page 102 of the Course Book and go over it briefly in class. A project evaluation and feedback document are printed at the back of this book. You can use these to give feedback to students.

Unit summary

1 **Answers:**
  a) general
  b) background
  c) aims
  d) subject
  e) real-world
  f) text
  g) research
  h) results
  i) thesis
  j) definition

3 **Possible answers:**
because they help you to organize your presentation / help you to remember the key points that you want to make

4 **Answers:**
A poster presentation must be clear and <u>concise</u>. The main point must be immediately clear to your <u>audience</u>, so you need to think carefully about <u>impact</u>. You must be selective – if you try to communicate too many ideas, your <u>main point</u> will be lost.

5   Possible answers:

a) Use headings to guide your reader. / Number headings correctly.

b) Make sure you acknowledge all references.

c) Arrange your bibliography appropriately. / Make sure it is in alphabetical order.

d) Exchange your project with a classmate for language checking.

e) Check that each section is linked to the previous and following one.

f) Check that your introduction and conclusion are linked to your title.

g) Make sure you have reacted to previous feedback.

Web resources

LEO writing abstracts

This page reviews abstract writing. It lists the steps of writing an abstract and provides an example abstract.

http://leo.stcloudstate.edu/bizwrite/abstracts.html

Poster presentations: article by Student Learning Centre, University of Auckland, New Zealand

Some additional information about designing a poster presentation, e.g., use of pictures and colour.

http://www.uk-student.net/modules/wfsection/article.php?articleid=163

University of Canberra: tips for oral presentation

Comprehensive list of tips on how to design, organize and structure academic presentations. It also gives useful language and advice about body language, handouts, etc.

http://learnonline.canberra.edu.au/mod/resource/view.php?inpopup=true&id=125956.

University of Richmond: writer's web

This site is complex in places, but it has some interesting and innovative ideas on how to approach different stages in the writing process, including editing and peer-editing. You can explore the topics by looking at the writer's web mind map and clicking on the area that interests you.

http://writing2.richmond.edu/writing/wweb.html

Additional online activities

Additional interactive activities to accompany this unit can be found online, at www.englishforacademicstudy.com.

Example note cards

The retail trade in China: why native enterprises often fail

a) Foreign competition

b) Lack of government support

c) Financing + funding problems

d) Recession

Modern migration and its economic impact

Receiving countries	Sending countries
a) Competition with local labour	a) Loss of investment
b) Reduced wages	b) Labour shortages
c) Employment vacancies filled	c) Increased development problems

The causes and effects of climate change in recent years

Causes	Effects
• Global warming	• Ecological damage
• El Niño	• Land loss
• Human activity	• Global cooperation

Appendix 1: Written project evaluation

Name:	Overall grade:
Title:	

Grades for individual aspects of the project (details overleaf)

Content	
Use of source material	
Organization	
Language	

Presentation of material

		Tick below as appropriate
Well-presented	Contains all appropriate sections, e.g., title page, abstract, headings in main body, appropriate font, bibliography.	
Presentation needs development	For example, not enough headings, inappropriate font, missing bibliography/references at end.	

Learner independence

		Tick below as appropriate
Appropriate	Asks for help/advice when necessary or appropriate, but otherwise is capable of working on her/his own.	
Needs to develop	At times independent, but tendency to be too dependent on tutor.	
Inadequate	Does not show the ability to work on her/his own, but fails to ask for help **or** can only complete project under pressure from tutor.	

Comments:

Photocopiable

Tutor:

Photocopiable handout

Content

Clearly focused content, relevant to title. Length, scope and level of detail are appropriate/relevant. Arguments are well presented and developed, with supporting evidence from a variety of sources. Shows awareness of complexities of the topic.	A
Generally well-focused content. May be lacking in level of detail or development of ideas and/or limited in scope (which may affect length). Much of the content may be descriptive, when a critical approach is required. Some understanding of complexities of topic evident. Argument may be inconsistent or insufficiently developed.	B
Focus at times waivers; some content may be irrelevant. Clearly limited in level of detail, superficial treatment of subject, with no development of ideas. Shows lack of awareness of complexities of topic. May be very short. Little or no evidence of evaluation of ideas, staying mostly at the descriptive level. No clear line of argument.	C
No obvious focus; clearly content inadequately researched; unable to deal with topic (probably very short) **or** wholesale plagiarism has made it impossible to assess true level. Too much personal/anecdotal material.	D

Use of source material

Effective use of a range of sources, appropriate incorporation through paraphrase/quotations/summary. Shows ability to synthesize well from several sources to support ideas. Bibliography and referencing follow academic convention, and a range of sources are used. No obvious/conscious plagiarism.	A
Effective use of sources, mostly when summarizing/paraphrasing ideas clearly. Shows some evidence of synthesis of information. Bibliography and use of sources show an understanding of the concept of referencing, though this is not always followed, e.g., bibliography missing publisher/not in alphabetical order; references in text include first name/title. No obvious/conscious plagiarism.	B
Limited sources used, and summary/paraphrase of ideas not always clear. Some attempt at synthesis of ideas. Clearly has problems compiling bibliography and incorporating sources in an appropriate way, although there is some attempt to do this. Poor language control may be a factor. Suspicion of plagiarism in some sections.	C
Inadequate attempt to use source material, e.g., may only use one source or none. Content based mainly on student's view with no evidence to support it. Shows little understanding of the importance of referencing and academic conventions. No bibliography or, where this exists, does not follow appropriate academic convention. No reflection of course content.	D

Organization*

Overall structure and main ideas are clearly organized and easy to follow. Introduction outlines structure of project and has clear thesis. Conclusion is clear, with evidence of evaluation of the work. Ideas are effectively linked together and 'flow' coherently and cohesively, with appropriate headings in text, making it easy for the reader to follow.	A
Overall structure and main ideas are generally obvious. Introduction and/or conclusion may not be appropriately linked to main body. Lack of headings in some sections hinders reader. At times a tendency to move from one idea to another with no attempt to link them.	B
Difficult for reader to establish overall structure/identify main ideas. May be due to poor language control, which also affects cohesion. Introduction/conclusion may be inadequate. Frequent move from one idea to another, with no attempt to link them.	C
Ineffective attempt to organize the work. Very difficult for reader to follow the text. The introduction fails to give the reader an overview/clear idea of what will follow **or** wholesale plagiarism has made it impossible to assess true level.	D

Language

Complex ideas clearly expressed, with wide, accurate usage of vocabulary and grammar; any errors do not impede communication. Appropriate academic style, with good grasp of hedging, etc. Use of a wide range of connectors to link ideas at paragraph and sentence level.	A
Ideas on the whole clearly expressed. Linking of ideas within paragraphs generally appropriate, but at times lacking between sections. Some vocabulary and/or grammar problems, but generally these do not impede communication. Spelling and/or punctuation may lack control, although this generally does not interfere with comprehension.	B
Some ideas are simply expressed, but other ideas are not clearly expressed. No evidence of ability to express complex ideas. Linking between and within sentences may be inconsistent. Fairly serious vocabulary and/or grammar problems; can impede communication. Spelling and/or punctuation may be fairly seriously flawed. May be too much use of lists rather than continuous prose.	C
The level of vocabulary and grammar is so consistently weak and the spelling/ punctuation so poor that the end product fails to achieve its purpose due to ineffective communication (or wholesale plagiarism has made it impossible to assess true level).	D

*Refer to the *Language* section for some aspects of *Organization*

Appendix 2: Presentation assessment

Name:

Title:

Overall grade:

Tutor:

	Profile A	Profile B	Profile C	Profile D
Delivery	Pronunciation hardly interferes with comprehension. Volume and speed are appropriate. Rhythm and intonation are varied and appropriate. Good eye contact.	Pronunciation of individual words occasionally interferes with comprehension. Volume and speed are adequate. Rhythm and intonation generally appropriate. Eye contact may be limited.	Pronunciation of chunks of language at times makes comprehension impossible. Volume/speed may be inadequate, and there is little or no eye contact. May be inappropriate use of gesture.	Pronunciation and intonation frequently impede comprehension, making it difficult to evaluate the presentation. May be inaudible.
Language	Clear evidence of ability to express complex ideas, using a wide range of appropriate vocabulary. Cohesive devices, where used, contribute to fluency. High degree of grammatical accuracy.	Some ability to express complex ideas, although not consistently. Reasonable use of range of vocabulary and structures. Cohesive devices, where used, contribute to fluency, but are sometimes misapplied.	Range of vocabulary and structures are adequate to express simple ideas. Errors sometimes impede communication.	Very limited range of vocabulary and grammar means ideas are expressed with difficulty. Presentation is often repetitive, due to insufficient control of language.
Organization	Strong introduction, with clear outline. Logical ordering of main points. Effective conclusion.	Generally, there is a logical ordering of main ideas. Introduction/conclusion are linked with main points.	Presentation lacks clear organization of ideas, making it difficult to follow.	Lack of any apparent organization makes it difficult to follow presentation.
Content	Content is appropriate and relevant. Topic is explored in sufficient depth.	Content is mostly appropriate and relevant.	Content is at times irrelevant, and development of ideas is superficial.	Content is not always related to the topic and there is little development of ideas.
Evidence of preparation	Evidence of thorough familiarity with topic. Fluent delivery, with skilful use of notes. Deals well with questions. Use of PowerPoint/OHTs enhances the presentation.	Familiar with topic. Use of notes sometimes interferes with delivery of presentation. Use of PowerPoint at times distracts from presentation content, due to unclear script/ inappropriate pictures/poor timing.	Reasonable preparation. Organization mostly clear and logical. Acceptable use of visual aids. Some difficulty in dealing with questions.	Inadequate preparation, with little evidence of familiarity with subject. Visual aids unhelpful, unclear or ineffective. Too much focus on PowerPoint rather than basic content. Inability to deal with questions.

Comments: